9 LESSONS FOR A MEANINGFUL LIFE

J.K. DENNIS

9 LESSONS FOR A MEANINGFUL LIFE

Voices of Inspiration

3HP
Three House Publishing

Three House Publishing
P.O. Box 6672
Chesterfield, MO 63006, U.S.A
www.3HP.us

Copyright © 2005 by J.K. Dennis
First Edition
Printed in the U.S.A

All rights reserved. No part of this book may be reproduced, stored in a retrieval system, or transmitted by any form or by any means, electronic, mechanical, photocopying, recording, or otherwise, except as may be expressly permitted by the applicable copyright statutes or in writing to Three House Publishing.

"Billy" first appeared as "Why I Married Essie" in *Obsidian II*, 1997.
"Earl" first appeared as "Dead Man's Walk" in *Lonzie's*, 1999.

Library of Congress Control Number: 2005901622
ISBN 0-9766429-0-5

Cover design by Peg Lestina

PUBLISHER'S NOTE
This is a work of fiction. The names, characters, places, and incidents either are the product of the author's imagination or are used fictitiously, and any resemblance to actual persons, living or dead, events, or locales is entirely coincidental.

For my students

Contents

Lesson 1: "You can't teach an old dog new tricks. But you can teach old tricks to a new dog." —Cyrus 1

Lesson 2: "Time can heal your wounds but not your scars." —Grace 11

Lesson 3: "You can do anything if you try it first and think about it later." —Billy 26

Lesson 4: "If somebody remembers you, you never die." —Mattie 37

Lesson 5: "Give a man a fish and you will feed him for a day. Teach a man how to fish and you will feed him for a lifetime. When all the fish are gone, he can start raising chickens." —Abel 47

Lesson 6: "You can chase love up the road and back while happiness is on your doorstep." —Rachel 73

Lesson 7: "Don't lose the race you aren't supposed to win." —Earl 83

Lesson 8: "Run your own life or somebody else will." —Odessa 94

Lesson 9: "The life you save may be your own." —Sonny and Cleophus 105

When one is on the soil of one's ancestors, most anything can come to one.

—JEAN TOOMER

9 LESSONS FOR A MEANINGFUL LIFE

Cyrus

ALMOST EVERY DAY, somebody walks into my store asking about a job. If I could ask one thing in return, I'd ask, are you a Christian? It ain't like me to go and hire Tom, Dick, or Harry at the drop of a dime. Since life hasn't always been easy for me or for half the folks I know here in Moon County, Georgia, I thought I should tell you that I built this little grocery store from the ground up, but don't let the small size of it fool you. My store might not be as big as old Potter's, but it has made me a pretty content man as far as money goes. I must have stacked over one million canned goods in my lifetime and I expect to stack many more before it's all over for me. You have to remember to turn the cans so the label faces the front, or the lazy folks will complain that it's hard to tell the beans from the peas.

I believe in knowing folks. I know about everybody here in Moon County, and I get a chance to talk to half the population every week. A job like mine requires you to talk a lot, but there are times when I don't say one word. I keep my mouth shut tighter than a rat trap. In fact, I think it's probably a good thing when folks don't say anything at all. A lot of folks come in on Fridays because that's payday at the cotton mill. You can't let them boss you, especially if it is one of those days when you've decided you're better off keeping quiet. If folks ask me why I'm not talking, I ignore them. I put their groceries in the bag and let them pick up one of those trash magazines that talks about love affairs and folks seeing Jesus in places like Omaha. Honestly, I don't understand how folks can move a pencil to write some of the mean things they write and then have the nerve to add the name of Jesus to it. I wonder why folks would want to do something mean to a good man's name.

Like I was saying, I don't hire any Tom, Dick, or Harry at the drop of a dime. Tobias Cutter used to work here. He had to quit, though. Tobias never said much of anything to anybody. I thought he was the quiet type. You might hear some folks say I fired him, but that's just a falsehood. If you don't believe anything else about me, I want you to believe that I give folks chances because I'm a good man at heart. Tobias is in the jailhouse now, and he might spend the rest of his life in the Sparta State Prison. I haven't found anybody to take his place. I need to because I'm in my bullfrog years and I can't do all the work around here myself. The canned goods in the back need to be stacked on the shelves. The apples and oranges need to be put out on display and the floors need to be swept. When folks see dirt on the floor, it makes them not want to spend their money. Everything else is what I call "learn-as-you-go."

I think everybody on this earth has the potential to do something good in life. I used to tell Tobias that all the time. I don't think he ever listened to me. That is exactly what is wrong with the folks in Moon County…they won't pay you two cents worth of attention if what you have to say doesn't line up with love affairs and folks seeing Jesus in places like Omaha.

Most folks around Moon County claim to be Christians, but the church I used to go to doesn't even exist anymore. Some folks still believe lightning struck and caused it to burn to the ground because of the stories reporters wrote about Jesus. Those magazines sold quicker than cheap diamonds. Folks came in, got a long neck cola drink, and stood in front of the store with their faces tucked between the pages. I bet not a single one of them ever read the Bible from cover to cover. Of course, it is a difficult piece of reading. I read every now and again when business is slow. I allow my employees to do e-d-u-c-a-t-i-o-n from time to time. If the judge decides not to send him to the Sparta State Prison, I'm hoping Tobias Cutter will walk through that door knowing the meaning of every word in the used dictionary I sent to the jailhouse just for him.

My wife's name is Myrtle, and she has a sister named Alice. Alice gave me that used dictionary for Christmas last year, and I kept it under the counter before I gave it to Tobias. Let me tell you something about Alice. The place in her head where they were supposed to use screws…well, somebody used thumbtacks, and that is why Alice is crazy on Mondays and Saturdays. She comes in on one of her crazy days and does her best to put everything on credit like she does when she goes to old Potter's store. You've got to have a spine with her, seeing how she is a slow learner. You have to make a person like Alice understand that family ties don't always work, and that you're not some Tom, Dick, or Harry hired at the drop of a dime.

Let me be the first to tell you that q-u-a-l-i-t-y goes a long way with me. I tried to make Tobias look the word up, but I couldn't get him to open that dictionary for anything on this side of Moon County. He said there were more important things to do in life besides look up words in a dictionary, but it only takes about a minute. I guess he is regretting that now. Life will make you regret a lot of things. That's why you've got to do right the first time around or you'll be messed up until the day you die.

That's why I started going to church, before folks said lightning struck it and burned it down. I bet it might be hard for you to imagine lightning striking a church. It was hard for me too. All I could do was watch those flames light up a dark rainy night. Nobody except Reverend James said one word. I have lived in Moon County all my life, and I used to think folks here were the talking types, like me, but that night, it was so quiet I could hear the rain beating against my face. When most folks come to my store, one or two might ask me what I thought really happened that night, but I don't say one word. I keep my mouth closed tighter than a can of corn. It's hard to get a secret out of me when I'm playing the mule. The sad part of the whole story is that it's taking a long time to rebuild our church. I heard it was because we didn't have enough money. That wasn't hard for me to believe because Reverend James up and left with the insurance money.

The Reverend and I used to have little talks from time to time. He'd come in and stand right over by the register dressed in his suit and hat, as usual. The Reverend never liked to touch doorknobs or shake hands with us common folks. He used his handkerchief or wore gloves to protect what he called his holy hands. We'd make conversation, trying to see who could get the most words in the air. Reverend James has been divorced twice. His third wife is a young girl named Ruby and he won't let Ruby out of his sight for anything on this side of Moon County. Every now and again, he brought her into the store with him. She never said more than two words, hello and good-bye. You couldn't get Tobias to work right when Ruby came into the store. The Reverend would give Tobias a list of groceries to get together while we talked. Every time he had to pass Ruby, Tobias tripped over his own feet like he had weak legs or something. One time, I thought I saw Tobias wink at Ruby. After that, the only time I ever saw Ruby again was in church on Sundays.

One day, Ed Lawson came into the store before Reverend James arrived. Ed bought a long neck cola drink. There are a few things you ought to know about old Ed Lawson. I can tell you all about him and what he used to do when he came to church. Ed used to come to Sunday service and take his shoes off and sleep just like he was on a Florida vacation. He's the president of the Gentlemen's Society here in Moon County. It's a club for men who like to get drunk, tear up the county, and chase loose women. Every now and again, they help society by giving ten dollars to the senior student who writes the best composition. Last year, Ed made himself one of the judges, and everybody knew he could hardly spell his own first name. When Ed drinks too many cola drinks, he'll give you the whole pedigree of the Gentlemen's Society and tell some of their secrets. The Gentlemen's Society has been around for years, and if you must know, I wouldn't join for a million dollars.

By the looks of things, you'd never know Ed was in some kind of Gentlemen's Society. He mostly dressed in overalls and you couldn't catch him without a toothpick in his mouth. He'd come in here and grab a long neck cola drink out of the ice box and grab one of those trash magazines, fold it, and put it under his arm. Then we'd go sit in front of the store and talk. He'd tell me all about the Gentlemen's Society because he has always tried to get me to join. You'd be pretty amazed at how they go about initiating new members. I heard that one of the things they do is get you drunk on homemade gin, then paddle your backside just to see if you are a man who is good enough to be voted in. But Ed said from his own mouth that I shouldn't believe that because it was just a falsehood. Ed told me they have to wear those cone hats with a tassel because of tradition. He told me that they go somewhere besides Moon County when they really wanted to have a good time, but if you wake up one morning and the mailbox is all busted up, you should not be surprised if it turns out that somebody in the Gentlemen's Society did it.

Ed told me none of the men in the Gentlemen's Society knew one thing about what happened to our church. Ed and his folks have been members of the church for as long as I can remember. Ed told me he was hurt folks would even think somebody in the Gentlemen's Society could do such a terrible thing. He said he was trying hard to repent, so he wouldn't end up in hell when he died.

Then Ed opened up that trash magazine he had tucked under his arm and we both agreed it was a shame the way those reporters disgraced the Son of God. But he read on. I used to believe Ed was a good man, so I asked him if he ever heard a voice whispering in his ear when nobody else was around. He told me that he did, but he didn't know who it was. I told Ed that I heard a voice whispering to me all the time and that I thought it was God. Ed said he never thought about it like that, but I was probably right. Then Ed asked me if I had ever read the Bible from cover to cover. I told him that I was trying to, but certain parts like Revelation just gave me the fits because I couldn't figure out the meaning. It shocked me to the core when Ed said that Revelation meant that the Savior was coming down from heaven to make this world a better place for everybody.

So, Reverend James walks into the store just minutes after Ed left. I tell the Reverend exactly what took place between me and Ed and he can't believe that I'm friendly with a backslider like Ed Lawson. Ed said the Gentlemen's Society and most of the regular good folks claim they didn't know what happened to the church. Reverend James didn't believe me. He said that Ed knew the truth and he wasn't going to tell it because he was known to admit to doing real bad things when he drank too much gin. The Reverend also told me that if I didn't want to end up in the asylum, I had better stop telling folks that God whispered in my ear. Ed said I was probably right. Then Reverend James told me I needed to read the Bible more and stop talking to that devil, Ed Lawson. But I told him that Ed did more talking to me and that I was just a listener. But he said that was worse. So when he left that day, I felt awfully bad and took aims to keep my mouth shut and repent again. But you and I both know that repenting ain't as easy as some folks say it is.

Personally, I didn't see anything so terrible about telling folks that God whispered in my ear. It wasn't like I was going around claiming to be one of those disciples you read about in the Bible. I have my flaws, as Reverend James called them. I admit I don't much like stacking canned goods every week. I admit I take a sip of gin every other night. Sometimes, when I tell

Myrtle that I'm going fishing, I go find myself a cool shady place out by the Oconee River and drink myself dizzy. I admit that I even cheated on Myrtle, but I only did it once and I later found out that she knew about it anyway. I told her about God whispering in my ear and she said that if God whispered to me there was hope for me after all. I could become a born again Christian.

It was Myrtle who made me go to church. I didn't want to pay tithes, but Myrtle said that I should because I had a lot of sins. So, I went to church pretty regular in a suit and one of the ties that Myrtle bought me for Christmas. I paid my tithes. I said my prayers. I still had the gin hidden in the back of the coat closet so Myrtle couldn't find it and fuss at me. If she did, I'd just go out and fish in the Oconee River. Nobody bothered me when I went there. Sitting out there alone, I could hear God whispering in my ear all day long. Most times he said, "You're a good man, Cyrus." I figured that was the one thing he wanted me to remember because that's what he always told me. I understood simple words much better than the words in the Bible. But now that we don't have a church or a reverend, I don't read the Bible anymore. I read my dictionary instead. I guess you're probably thinking I'm i-n-c-o-r-r-i-g-i-b-l-e.

Maybe you can't see that the church meant a lot to folks in Moon County. All that Bible stuff Reverend James talked about started to make sense to me after a while. But whenever I talked to him, and I explained back to him what I read in the Bible, he'd say my meanings were all wrong and he'd change them around. Then he'd tell me I needed to study my Bible more and stop taking God's name in vain. So I'd get mad and tell him he was going against my way of seeing things. Then he'd tell me that was no way to be talking to a man who always walked in the footsteps of Jesus.

Well, a few days later, folks were running down the road in the rain screaming and hollering about how our church was burning. I wouldn't have believed it if so many folks weren't out so late at night. And there it was, burning right there in front of me. That was the first time in my life I can remember not being able to say one word. All I could do was wonder what Jesus might have to say about the whole thing. I don't expect he'd say what Reverend James said to me that night. I stood right beside him and helped him pull himself together. He could throw fits worse than an old grandma at a funeral. Then everything got as quiet as a graveyard, and Reverend James leaned over, put his head on my shoulder, and whispered, "Well, Cyrus, I guess everybody's hope is gone now."

After the church burned down, newspaper reporters started making tracks behind Ed Lawson and the Gentlemen's Society everywhere they went. Everybody in Moon County knows that reporters are worse than flies. That picture of Ed and the Gentlemen's Society has been in the newspaper for days because those reporters did what they called an exposé on the Gentlemen's Society, saying it did more harm to the community than anything else. Ed's poor wife, Louise, had a nervous breakdown after some folks had a big rally in front of their house, calling for Ed to step down as the president of the Gentlemen's Society or leave Moon County. Myrtle told me Louise told her those reporters are still around here in disguise, and not to be fooled the way she was, because they're all a bunch of backstabbers. The whole Gentlemen's Society is sitting over there in the jailhouse with Tobias, waiting to see just who was going to have to do time for crime in the Sparta State Prison.

What I don't understand is how, after the church burned down, bits and pieces of the truth came out. First, a big rumor came out about how Tobias Cutter and Ruby were having some love affair like something you read in a trash magazine. Then folks started saying Ruby could never go anywhere by herself, because Reverend James wouldn't let her. Nobody believed the story except the folks who didn't have anything else to believe in. Plus, I told Myrtle that Tobias worked right here in my store, and I never saw any signs of love in him and he never said one word about a love affair. Sure, I asked him about it a million times. But he said all that talk was r-i-d-i-c-u-l-o-u-s. Then Myrtle said I didn't know folks as well as I thought I did. But I don't care who you know or where you go, if there is a rumor out there somewhere, you can bet your last paycheck that you got a few folks here in Moon County playing detective. Sure enough, folks say Reverend James had to go to one of those church retreats he was always going to. Ruby usually went, and Deacon Charlie Crawford got to play Reverend for a day. Ruby claimed she was too sick to go. She was sick all right! The Reverend said he forgot his good Bible, so he had to turn around and come back, and guess who the Reverend saw climbing out of his window? Tobias Cutter! It turned out that Tobias was trying to get into The Gentleman's Society. As a part of his initiation, Ed and the rest of the Gentlemen's Society told him he had to do something crazy, like have some love affair with a married woman. Tobias had to keep quiet about the whole thing or else they would never make him a member. So being young and foolish, Tobias picked Ruby out of all the women in Moon County.

A few days later, a big thunderstorm hit Moon County, our church went up in smoke, and the sheriff said that Tobias and the men in the Gentlemen's Society swore on the Bible that Reverend James set the church on fire for revenge. At first, nobody wanted to believe a word they said, including me. Then, all of a sudden, Reverend James left with Ruby and the insurance money and speculation was turned loose.

After folks noticed that Reverend James was gone, things changed in Moon County. On Sundays, folks have a choice of either sleeping late or crowding up Deacon Charlie Crawford's living room to listen to him mess up Bible scriptures. But me, I just take a bucket of worms, a fishing pole, and a dictionary and head to the Oconee River to talk to God one-on-one. Myrtle bought me one of those pocket-sized dictionaries. She thought it might help lift my spirit. I was surprised because I didn't know they made dictionaries so darn small. There is not a day that you'd catch me without it tucked away in one of my pockets.

Myrtle and I never had any children of our own, and I used to think of Tobias as the son I never had. But now I see it was best that I see him as a friend. I don't want you to think that friends are above firing in my store. I treat everybody like equals around here, but before I hire anybody to take Tobias's place, I want that person to look straight into my eyes so I can see if he's a Christian or not. If he is, I will have to watch him real close.

Grace

I find the love letter that this woman name Lorraine write to my husband Dipsey. He forget to put the lock on his trunk before he leave to go fish in the Oconee River.

All day, I think about her. Is she handsome? Tall? Stout? Clean?

How she dress? How she wear her hair? Is she church going?

She say she like it when Dipsey on top of her. I wonder if he make her feel something inside her heart. I wonder if she like me, and don't feel nothing at all sometimes.

Dipsey never seem to care much about how I feel. He can be blind to what he don't want to see. That's how come I know he will never see that me and Lorraine are more alike than he think.

Dipsey come around late fall and say he be needing a wife to settle down with. He ask my momma if he can marry me. She hand me over to him with a few dresses in a potato sack.

Dipsey older than me. I'm fifteen, and I don't menstruate. Momma say it will come later. I tell Momma I don't love him. She say it will come later.

After two months, Momma get sick and die and we bury her next to Daddy. The Reverend let me read a poem at the funeral. It's a death poem. I keep it in the Bible. I go to read it one day, and it's not there. Dipsey say he took it, and I never see it again.

I try to put together what I remember. The harder I try, the less I remember. I think about the flower print dress that I wore to the funeral. That dress be the only thing that feel right about life to me.

My flower print dress be my only good dress. Momma make the dress for my wedding. I think it be the prettiest dress I ever own. It's got so much of Momma in it. Sometimes when I wear it, I can feel her. Her touch soft like a feather pillow.

Momma give me a notebook for my present. I fill it with poems and put it in the chifforobe under the nightdress that always smell like talc. Most of the poems be about rain and clouds because that's how I feel around Dipsey. One day, I'm rain; the next day, I'm clouds. I go to get my notebook one morning. I search under my nightdress. Dipsey say he took it and I never see it again. Thinking about Gertie Talbert be the one thing that help me get murder off my mind. Dipsey never know she be the one who save him.

I ask him to buy me a new dress because he say my flower print dress be the ugliest dress he ever seen, and it ain't proper for his daddy funeral. He say he rather rot than spend a dime of his money on a dress for me. He say my momma should have learned me how to make dresses.

I say I write poems. Dipsey frown, and say he don't need a scribbling wife. He say he should have married Iris Baker because at least she know how to make her own dresses. So I try to be Iris.

Iris the seamstress who go with Mr. Peeler. She smart and pretty. She lecture me on style and learn me how to walk with a book on my head. She alter my flower print dress for free until I learn sewing proper.

One day, I read her a poem I write, and she hand me the page she tear out the magazine about a poem contest with a hundred dollar prize. I feel like there be something in the world for me to live for.

When I tell Dipsey about the contest and the prize money, he frown and ask me who going to pay me a hundred dollars for scribbling. He push a piece of bacon in his mouth and turn the page of the newspaper. He never look at the love poem on the table next to the fork and knife. I watch it soak up the little drops of coffee he spill on it. The poem be dead before it ever have a chance to live.

I wash the dishes while he read the newspaper.

I say a prayer and I think about Iris.

Iris shorten the sleeves on my dress for me. I want to try the dress on, but Dipsey honk the horn of the motorcar, and I leave Iris standing in her new house complaining about making new curtains and Gertie husband, Harlem.

Going home, I get up the nerve to ask Dipsey to teach me how to drive the motorcar, so I can go where I want to go. He say I'll run out all the gas driving back and forth to Iris house. Besides church, Iris house be the one place Dipsey let me go without making a fuss.

The ladies at church say how good my flower print dress look with short sleeves.

Iris walk in on the arm of Mr. Peeler. She wear a fur stole and a dress with feathers on it. Mr. Peeler buy the fur stole just for her. He have the money to buy the things that Dipsey think be too wasteful. Iris and Mr. Peeler sit next to us.

Gertie walk in and sit down in front of us. Harlem not with her.

Dipsey say stop staring at Gertie.

I stop staring, but Gertie stay in my mind. I wonder why she start wearing those big floppy hats. I wonder why I never notice her before Iris mention her. Why she always sitting by herself? Why can't I hold back my thoughts on her? I see the tears come down her face. Tears come down my face too.

I tell Dipsey that I want to write a poem about Gertie for the contest. He frown, then shake his head.

When I go to Iris house, I tell her what I told Dipsey. She say, "Pay no attention to Dipsey, Grace. You can write a poem about anything that suits you. If you want to write a poem about Gertie Talbert, then you write one."

"Why can't Dipsey be nice to me for a change?"

"Honey, folks would be breaking down my front door if I had the answer to that question. At least you ain't got it as bad as Gertie."

"What's wrong with Gertie?"

"Harlem driving her crazy with his ways. Who do you think is the daddy of Hazel Rogers newborn child?"

"Him?"

"Umm hum. Now imagine how Gertie must feel about that. You know how folks talk around Moon County."

"Why can't the men be more like Mr. Peeler?"

"Honey, Peeler ain't much better. You know he ask me to marry him."

"What did you say?"

"What do you think I said? No!"

"You don't like Mr. Peeler?"

"I like him. I just don't want to marry him. I'd only end up sharing him with some woman he got up in Atlanta, and God knows where else. You know he want to buy the old Wilson house, fix it up, and resale it for a higher price."

"Mr. Peeler a smart one, huh?"

"No, he just a traveling businessman who love women too much. I don't care how many times men like him tell you they love you, they always be the ones you end up sharing with another woman. I had enough of that with George."

"You mean George cheated on you?"

"Honey, he got two grown boys by some woman over in Sparta County. They every spit of George. They all come to his funeral."

"You never mention anything about them."

"Honey, it ain't the type of thing a woman want to holler to the world, especially when her own barrel been empty all these years. George always did want some boys though."

"No woman would ever want Dipsey. I don't even want him. Hair grow on his toes."

"Honey, you'd be surprised. Look around you. All you see is women and children. The rooster got his pick of the hens these days. It's a pretty terrible thing when you think about it. But then again, the world a pretty terrible place. Ain't nothing guaranteed. Thank God for insurance. Dipsey got good insurance?"

"I don't know."

"What do you mean you don't know?"

"I don't know. Dipsey say that be menfolk business."

"Honey, these the things a wife ought to know. You young wives never ask the right questions."

"Dipsey get mad when I ask too many questions. I ain't been married to him one whole year and already it seem like forever."

"Honey, one day you will look in the mirror and start thinking marriage longer than forever. Now step up on this stool and let me pin a higher hem."

IRIS SAY I'D be able to show my legs more with a higher hem. Dipsey say I got legs like a chicken. They don't stay that way. My body fill out more after Dipsey, Jr. come. The labor last four hours. Sweet Flora, the midwife, say she don't think the baby ready to come. But Iris don't believe her. She don't let go of my hand until Dipsey, Jr. born to the world.

Iris say the baby look like Dipsey, but I say he more like a poem. He my pride and joy, and the same for Dipsey too. Dipsey sometimes beat me to the cradle when Dipsey, Jr. cry. Sometimes, he call him his son, like he got more relation to the child than I do.

Dipsey, Jr. grow up real fast. There be days when I can still feel him sleeping in my arms. There be days when I cry because I know he really not my first child. I will never know what would have come of that child. Dipsey, Jr. a lawyer now and say all his words proper. He make me and Dipsey sound backward when we talk. We be too shame to say much when we go up on the train to visit. We don't talk Chicago. He move there and marry a handsome woman who look like she be fit for picture shows. They raising twins. One boy. One girl.

Every time Dipsey, Jr. send me letters, Dipsey want to know all about the children and the cases that he win. I wonder if Lorraine got any children, and whether any of them belong to Dipsey. She never mention children in her letter. If she got any, I hope they make her as proud as Dipsey, Jr. make me.

I find it hard to believe that Dipsey and Lorraine together around the time when Dipsey, Jr. was born. Something say to me he wasn't with her then. After Dipsey, Jr. born, I notice sparks of love in Dipsey toward me. He don't hate me as much for not being that woman he dream up in his head.

He come home from work and lift the baby out my arms and he want to know about my day. He bring me candy and flowers like Lorraine say he do for her. Then one day, the flowers and the candy stop coming. I ask why. He say it be too wasteful. I ask him about his insurance papers. He say not to meddle in things that don't concern me.

After I cook Dipsey breakfast and get him off to work, I search every corner of the old shack house we rent. I search underneath the bed; I search the chifforobe; I search the trunk. It's full of clothes and shoes. I find his insurance papers. I also find glossy postcards that say Alabama on the front. All the postage on them got marks, but ain't no writing on the back. Then Dipsey beat me, and I wish I'd never found those postcards at all.

Iris ask, "Grace, what in the sweet name of Jesus did Dipsey beat you for?"

"He say I be meddling in his business too much."

"Honey, you poor thing. Look at your eye and those bruises around your neck. Why you want the collar taken off this dress?"

"I don't like the way it rub against my neck when I turn my head."

"Honey, when Dipsey get finish with you, you won't have a head. Things like this get worse long before they get better. Just look at Gertie."

"When you see her?"

"I see her in the five-n-dime. She had on one of those big floppy hats. But even that hat couldn't hide the two swollen eyes she had. The poor thing got more trouble on her shoulders than she can stand. We got to pray for her. Elma Bailey told me she hear Gertie might be pregnant."

"Then I'll write a baby poem and send it to her."

"Honey, who in the sweet name of Jesus got time to write a poem for Gertie Talbert? This ain't the kind of thing you write a poem about. You got to get on your knees and pray to God. Don't you know that Gladys Scout going around talking about the stork and Harlem in the same breath without any shame on her face? Now, you can't get more terrible than that."

"Why don't Gertie divorce Harlem? I want me a divorce from Dipsey."

"Honey, where you going to get money for a divorce?"

"I've got to win that poetry contest, that's all. Then I can get myself a divorce and leave that old shack house for good."

"Honey, you shouldn't put all of your hope in that contest. Nobody around these parts ever seem to win things like that."

"I can win with help from God."

"Then, you better start praying because it's starting to look like you got two choices with Dipsey. You either kill him or leave him. Since you young and ain't got any children, I think you should leave."

"Why?"

"Honey, no offense, but you not a bird with very bright feathers. I just can't see you pulling off a clean murder."

"I can, too, pull off a clean murder, and take every bit of that insurance money!"

"Insurance or not, I suggest you stick to poems and leave murder alone. Ain't nothing more terrible than seeing a woman in one of those jailhouse dresses. You know they make all the women do the jailhouse laundry. That will wear your fingers down to fat nubs."

"That won't be me. I'll be sitting somewhere with the hundred dollars I'll win from that contest."

"Young wives always full of cloudy dreams. It's a shame there's no such thing as insurance for dreams."

"I found some postcards from Alabama in Dipsey trunk. The postage got marks, but ain't no writing on the back."

"Honey, that's one of the main signs!"

"Signs of what?"

"That Dipsey got another woman somewhere over in Alabama. It won't be long before Dipsey having babies with her, if he ain't doing it already."

"He ain't."

"How you know, being locked up in that house scribbling about God knows what all day? I spent so much time sitting in the house sewing, half of the time I didn't know where George was or what he was up to. You see the price I paid."

"Dipsey won't do that to me."

"Honey, you shouldn't put all of your hope in that. Do you love Dipsey?"

"No, I hate him with a passion."

"Passion sure be a tricky thing these days. I got a passion for Peeler, but I don't love him. Sweet Jesus know I'd never marry the rascal."

"I don't love Dipsey. I never have. My momma told me to marry him."

"Well, you got two choices: Kill Dipsey or leave him."

"I can't kill him. That will be a sin on me."

"Honey, just a minute ago, you told me you could! Make up your mind."

"Did you kill George?"

"You know I told you that George died of a heart attack."

"Why should I believe you?"

"Honey, I loved George. How was I suppose to know I married a man with a bad heart?"

"I can't kill Dipsey."

"Well, if you don't kill him, he will kill you. Remember, Dipsey probably got your name somewhere on those insurance papers, too."

"Dipsey won't do anything like that. He promise my momma he would take care of me."

"Honey, it's what he ain't doing that will kill you. Let me show you how to get rid of that lace collar."

IRIS TELL ME not to leave the house in my dress until my bruises leave. I stay in for two weeks. I have plenty to do. I read the insurance papers, but I don't understand all the words. I cook the food. I wash the dishes. I scrub the floors. I wash and iron the clothes and I write poems about Gertie.

I sit at the kitchen table thinking about the poems in the chifforobe. I have to pick one for the contest. I can't. I love them all so much. I decide to take them with me to Iris house and let her help.

When I go to the chifforobe and look under my night dress, my notebook gone. I search everywhere except Dipsey trunk. He got a lock on it.

I run to Iris house in tears. She say the date for the contest a week away, and I still got time to write another one. But I can't. Dipsey take something away from me that I don't think I can get back.

I come home and I wait at the kitchen table. I watch the clock on the wall. I stare at the sunlight on the curtains. I wonder why the days seem so long one day and so short the next. I wonder how much more time it will take before I can breathe around Dipsey.

I put the blank paper on the table between the pencil and the knife that I use to try to get into the trunk. I wait and worry. I think of words to write, but I don't write them. I pray. The more I pray, the more the notion of murder rub against me.

I hear Dipsey at the door. My hands shake. Dipsey walk in the kitchen. He stare at me like it's something different about my face. He ask me why his dinner ain't ready.

I don't say nothing.
He ask me again.
I don't say nothing.
I feel the slap come down hard on my face. My mind dizzy and blood come out my nose and spot my paper. I look up and see Dipsey with my eyes, but in my mind, I see Gertie standing in the sunshine.
I grab the pencil instead of the knife.
I write the first line of Gertie poem.
It say I do not love you anymore.
I sit there staring at those words while tears roll down my face.
I never finish the poem, because there be so many other things I have to do. Dipsey cut his hand on one of the machines at the cotton mill where he work. He get only half pay while on leave. We don't have enough money to pay the rent. No time left for scribbling. I have to work.

Iris say, "Grace, working will be good for you. At least you will be able to buy yourself a decent dress now. Plus, you will get a chance to get out of the house and do something with yourself."

"But I write poems."

"Honey, who going to give you pay for scribbling? Peeler say Mrs. Beckham maid quit and she looking for a clean girl to take her place. I think you should go see her. Peeler can put in a good word for you."

"I don't want to clean up after some old woman. I do that for Dipsey."

"Dipsey ain't paying you. The stork bringing you an extra mouth to feed and you think things be hard for you now, just wait."

"I don't know if I want this child."

"Honey, what do you mean you don't know! It's your first child. It ain't like you got much of a choice."

"I do. Sweet Flora say she know a doctor over in Sparta County who can get rid of it."

"Honey, Sweet Flora so old she can barely think straight. A child ain't something you can just get rid of without taking some time to think about it. You young. Imagine how you might feel years from now. One thing you don't want to do in life is look back with regret."

"A few months ago, you tell me to kill Dipsey. That ain't much different from killing a child. It's easier for me to kill this child inside of me than Dipsey. I know Dipsey."

"Honey, you need to feel it growing inside of you. Give yourself time is all I'm telling you. Think of the child. Your mind will change."

"No, it won't. My mind made already."

"Well, have you told Dipsey about this?"

"No, he don't know about it. He'll just complain about having another mouth to feed."

"It would be a shame if you didn't tell him. I bet his mind would change if you told him the stork was coming. I bet he'll stop beating on you too. Folks like dress patterns. They change all the time."

"I don't believe that."

"Where you going to get the money to pay this doctor over in Sparta County?"

"I thought you'd loan it to me. You say George left you all of that insurance money when he died. I'll pay you back every dime."

"It's never good to owe a debt you can't pay."

"I'll go talk to Mrs. Beckham tomorrow. I'll dig ditches for her if I have to."

"Honey, I can't help you and you know I would if I could."

"Why can't you?"

"Honey, that insurance money been gone. After I buried George and put the down payment on this house, there ain't nothing left. I thought I could afford this house. Then my sewing business got slow, and I couldn't make the notes. Peeler had to take over. This Peeler house now."

"Then I'll ask Peeler for the money."

"Honey, I don't think Peeler would ever give you the money for something like that. He love children to death. He got two, and neither one of them by his ex-wife."

"Well, I'll ask him. If he says no, then I'll work. I'll work myself to death before I have this child."

"Honey, talk to God. Just get down on your knees and talk to him. Ask him to guide your heart on the matter. He'll tell you what to do. You don't want to end up like me and Gertie, and have to pay a price you not strong enough to pay."

"What happen to Gertie?"

"Honey, nobody told you? Gertie killed Harlem last night. She stabbed him with an ice pick. It's a good thing she ain't pregnant, because she'll be locked up until the day she die."

"I don't want to be like Gertie."

"Honey, it's so easy to say that."

"But I don't!"

"Honey, you not a bird with strong wings. You can step down off that stool now; your dress look just fine to me. I don't think there's much else we can do to change it."

For luck, I wear my flower print dress when I go to Mrs. Beckham house to ask her about the job. Mrs. Beckham say Mr. Peeler tell her all about me. She look me over real good before she hire me.

Then I go to work. I cook her food. I wash her dishes. I scrub her floors. I'm lucky she pay somebody else to do the laundry, or I'd have to do that too.

My day off be on Tuesdays, because Mrs. Beckham need me to work on Sundays after church. I don't mind because I'm thankful for the job. I have to help Dipsey pay the rent, and I have to pay back the money Mr. Peeler loan me.

Mr. Peeler offer to drive me and Sweet Flora to Sparta County. He bring us home because Sweet Flora tell him I wouldn't be in any condition to walk. I promise him I will pay him every dime of his money. He tell me to get some rest.

Rest a word that Mrs. Beckham won't let me know. She got picky ways about her. After a few days, I got use to the way Mrs. Beckham like things done, and the bleeding finally stop just like Sweet Flora said it would.

Dipsey wasn't at home enough to notice me much. His hand got better, and then he back at work. He stop coming home for dinner. If he come home at all, he come in late at night and he leave early in the morning without eating breakfast.

There be nights when I can smell a woman perfume on him. I tell Iris that whoever the woman is, I hope she all Dipsey want her to be. Iris say I shouldn't worry myself over things like that. But I do.

Maybe, that be Lorraine perfume on Dipsey. Maybe, those be the years the two of them was together. Maybe, she let him get on top of her because he complain so much when I won't. Maybe, Dipsey like a poem to her. Maybe, he be the one thing that make her feel like there be something in the world for her to live for.

When I read the letter again, I think how Lorraine probably had Dipsey when I needed him the most. I tell him I don't like walking home from work in the dark. He don't make a fuss. He tell me I will be fine because no man would want me anyway.

I believe him. Then one night I don't believe him anymore.

Mr. Peeler drive by and see me walking by myself in the dark. He offer me a ride home.

I tell him I don't want to go home.

He ask me where I want to go.

I tell him he can take me anywhere besides home.

So he drive me out to the Oconee River.

Mr. Peeler park the car by the trees. He hold me. He kiss me. He tell me my lips sweeter than Iris lips.

For the first time in my life, I feel something in my heart for a man. It's the night I get pregnant with Dipsey, Jr. I want to have Mr. Peeler child. The child feel like the poem inside me that I never finish. I think a child will make Mr. Peeler love me because Iris say he love children. But he don't love me at all.

After I tell Mr. Peeler everything, he tell me that he'll take me to Sparta County. But I won't go. He try to make me go. But I won't go. Mr. Peeler move back to Atlanta and he take Iris with him. I forget love.

Mr. Peeler put the house up for sale for much less than Iris say it worth. Iris complain about moving so far from home. Dipsey say we would be fools if we don't buy Iris house. I tell him I like living in our old shack house.

But Dipsey don't listen to me.

I don't think I can live happy in Iris house. I don't think my mind will let me know any peace. I think that one day Dipsey will find out the truth and take Dipsey, Jr. away like he take my poems away. I live haunted.

I try to write poems. But that don't keep me from worrying.

Then one day, I'm sitting at the kitchen table sewing buttons on one of Dipsey shirts, and I think about my old flower print dress all folded and boxed somewhere in the attic. None of the dresses I buy from the store fit good. So I start making my own. I make so many dresses Dipsey ask me if I plan to sell some.

I tell him they not for sell and they not all for me. I tell him some of them be for Gertie. He tell me that if I want to spend all day making dresses for a woman who can't wear them sitting in prison, then that be fine with him.

He kiss me on my forehead. I smile. I've seen him walk out of the door with his fishing pool a thousand times. It's hard for me to hate somebody I know so much about. Why go back to living as rain one day and clouds the next when I didn't have to?

Like always, Dipsey ask me where I last see his lucky fishing hat just before he walk out the door. I laugh whenever he ask me that. It's sitting on the chair by the door, like always. I think Dipsey just like to hear me say those words. I laugh because there use to be a time when Dipsey wouldn't care about my words at all. Time still learning me and Dipsey some lessons. Now it's teaching us how to be the insurance for each other. Why should I let a letter change all that?

Dipsey come home from work one day and tell me Gertie died. I tell Dipsey that I'm going to make her a flower print dress like the one my momma made me. He sit across the kitchen table nodding and reading the newspaper. He look up and tell me that I'm doing the right thing for Gertie. He tell me that Gertie finally free. I smile because he right. I see Gertie dancing in my dreams sometimes.

Dipsey let me drive home from the funeral. He tell me that Gertie dress be the prettiest dress he ever seen. I cry because when he say that I feel something in my heart for him, and I think it be what love really suppose to feel like. Right then, I understand what Momma said so many years before.

My love for Dipsey did come later. It's not proud love. It's earned love. Maybe that be reason enough to forgive him.

BILLY

Since I couldn't get a job driving the ice truck, I went and got myself a job washing dishes at this new place that opened up in Moon County called Madame's Café. Miss DuMont came up from New Orleans and said Moon County was the plainest place she'd ever seen, and it needed some flavor. I walked up to the big sweaty woman and told her I needed a job. Buddy, who had worked before as a cook, persuaded her to go ahead and give me a chance, and she did. Buddy put me on the dishes, floors, and windows while he cooked and Miss DuMont sat at the table licking her fingers and separating dollars in piles. Madame's Café never made a whole lot of money, but my cut made me feel a whole lot richer than I was.

So I was cleaning windows the day Miss Shady Lady walked up Main Street carrying one of those little umbrellas. She had the most beautifulliest skin in the county. I gave her the name Miss Shady Lady because she carried that umbrella everywhere, rain or shine, and it cast a shadow over her head. She wore a lacy dress and one of those fancy hairstyles where the hair in the front waved off to the right. She had more fashion about herself than anybody I had ever seen. All the men tried to hold up traffic when they saw Miss Shady Lady coming. The womenfolk would slap their husbands because they couldn't help but to look. I thanked God I wasn't married; I could never have a woman slapping my face every time she found my eyes wandering off admiring sweet, pretty little things like Miss Shady Lady.

Miss Shady Lady came to Madame's Café one Wednesday. We weren't busy at all, but Miss DuMont was thumbing money as usual, and Buddy was cheating himself at some card game. There I was watching Miss Shady Lady sitting up there looking good in a lacy dress. She smelled like roses. I'm not talking about a little I'm-too-ashamed-to-open-up rose either. I'm talking about a fully-bloomed rose the color of blood and love. It smelled so good it made me forget it was a rose and made me think it was a woman with legs that stretched out for miles.

Miss Shady Lady had a book hiding that pretty face of hers, so I asked Miss DuMont could I take her a slice of cake and coffee. Miss DuMont went on and on about how I wasn't a waiter, and that my place was in the back, and my job was to tear down that stack of pots and pans that Buddy was always piling up like he was crazy. My hands wrinkled from so much dishwashing. Miss Shady Lady looked about in her prime thirties, and I didn't want age building any walls for me to climb over. So I cleared my throat and talked deep.

"Here is your order, Miss." She didn't even put that darn book down to take notice of me and how I was trying to do my best to make her feel at home like Miss DuMont said to.

"Thank you."

"You're welcome. Anything else I can get for you—like another piece of cake or something—you just let me know, okay?"

"I will."

"You like to read an awful lot?"

"Yes, I do," she said.

"It sure is a crime, the way you always allow that book there to hide that pretty face of yours," I told her.

"No, I don't," she said.

"If you need anything, don't be scared to holler."

"I got everything I need."

"You know, if you move over in that chair you won't have to worry about having the sun on your pretty skin. I see the way you hide under that umbrella you carry on your shoulders."

"It's a parasol."

"Oooooh, you know I thought that was what they called it. Let me tell you, right here this day, that I think that is the most beautifulliest parasol that I have ever seen."

"Thank you." Miss DuMont interrupted like only she could.

"Now, Billy, you don't get paid for socializing. Get back there and clean those dishes before I dock you one day's pay."

"I'm tired of washing dishes, Miss DuMont," I said, excusing myself from Miss Shady Lady. "Train me how to cook or something."

Buddy stood behind the counter laughing. Miss DuMont kept shuffling those one dollar bills like they were going to have babies or something.

"Billy, I can't have you around here burning up food and driving my customers away. Hell, I counted a loss here three times in a row, and we can't keep on having that."

"But still." I rubbed her shoulder to try to get her to see some of the light I was shining on the matter.

"I got an idea," said Buddy, throwing down the cards, "Let's run a special on chicken. Everybody in Moon County wants good fried chicken."

"That doesn't sound like a good idea to me. You stick with the cooking side and let me stick with the business side."

"What am I going to stick with?" I asked her.

"This floor we're standing on. What do you think I hired you for?"

Miss Shady Lady moved on out the door like she didn't want to disturb all the fussing. When she got outside, she flipped that little umbrella up and off she went, leaving that rose smell behind her.

I watched her walk away. Miss DuMont got up with the money gripped in her hand. She folded it over and stuffed it in the apron she was wearing. She didn't like using cash registers. She said machines and banks just couldn't be trusted after the stock market crashed.

"But still," I said.

"Look, Billy, you just clean those windows, keep the floor clean and shiny, and wash the pots and the pans. You heard me?"

"I heard you."

"I still think we should run a special," said Buddy.

"Who is going to clean chickens all day? It won't be me, no indeed. Like I told you before, chickens only bring a person bad luck," said Miss DuMont.

"Buddy and me have been talking, and we think we've got good heads for business, Miss DuMont. I think I could even be a pretty good cook if somebody learned me how."

"Billy, this ain't no school. Come on back here with me and let me get you started on those pots and pans."

Buddy started a new game with himself because nobody was in the café.

I walked on back to the kitchen where Miss DuMont stood by the sink thinking hard about something. I stood beside her lifting pots and pans. She looked over at me, and I half looked at her staring. She could be a real strange lady, especially when she went around mumbling and singing in that French talk, and dropping stuff in the pots that Buddy had cooking on the stove.

"Billy?"

"What?"

"Do you like that young lady who was just in here a minute ago?"

"Yeah, why?"

"Are you having a hard time getting her to like you back?"

"About as hard a time as they come, Miss DuMont."

"I have the secret on how you can make her yours for the rest of your life."

"What kind of secret?"

"There are some things you've got to do first."

"What things?"

"First, you've got to get yourself some garlic and a few hot peppers; then you have to kill a chicken and cut off the feet; then you make yourself a necklace and tie it around your neck. Let me take care of the rest. You heard me?"

"Yeah, but what is all that going to do, Miss DuMont?" I asked her.

"Let me worry about that. Do like I told you and I guarantee she'll be yours in due time."

"All right, but I thought you said killing chickens gave a person bad luck."

"It depends on the man doing the killing, Billy, that's all."

She gave me the garlic and some hot peppers. I killed a chicken and cut off the feet. Miss DuMont told me to take a needle and thread and sew them all together and then tie them around my neck. Of course, I didn't know the first thing about sewing, so I went right on over to Essie's house. Essie didn't have much fashion. She was just regular. She'd been cleaning house for Mrs. Beckham since we left school. But otherwise, Essie was just an at-home-kind-of-woman. She'd give me homemade caramel cakes on my birthdays, and she was the only person in Moon County who was happy I had found myself another job. She gave me a letter, and it said all kinds of nice things. Sometimes, she'd come to my house and cook, and we'd sit on the porch and smoke a cigar together.

"Hey, Essie, you didn't go to Mrs. Beckham's house today?"

"No, I quit because she cheated me out of my pay. What do you have in your hand that is smelling so God-awful-bad?"

"Stuff to get me a real lady." Essie's face lit up like the butt of a lightning bug. "I know you are good with a needle and thread and we have been knowing each other for a long time now. I was just wondering if you wouldn't mind helping me string together a necklace made out of garlic, peppers, and chicken feet."

"What is all of that stuff going to do, Billy?"
"Get me a lady, like I told you!"
"Really?"
"Yeah!"

Essie grabbed the parts for the necklace and started sewing. Poor Essie's nose ran so bad from the hot peppers, but she kept sewing and didn't complain one time. When Essie finished the necklace and tried to put it on me, one of the nails on the chicken foot scratched me on my neck. She took a few steps back, then said the whole thing was crazy, but the necklace didn't look too bad from a distance. Between the garlic and the peppers, I just couldn't get myself to function right.

My legs took me on to Madame's Café. My head was spinning and my eyes saw two of everything. I believed folks thought I was crazy the way I was shedding tears and reaching out for things like I was a blind man. When I made it to the café, Buddy told me that Miss DuMont had to go off on business, and we had to run the place until she could get back. Buddy asked me about the garlic and the peppers, and the necklace, and why I was crying like a baby and sweating like a pig.

"This is how I'm going to get Miss Shady Lady when she struts in here looking so fine and pretty and smelling so good!"

"You'd better go back there and wash all of those pots and pans," said Buddy.

"You use an awful lot of pots and pans for this place to be so empty all the time. Those pots and pans will just have to wait. I'm waiting on Miss Shady Lady first."

"I need extra pots and pans because I'm trying out some new recipes. But Miss DuMont never lets me cook what I want to cook. It is always what she wants. I've been saving to start my own café some day."

The necklace was getting tight around my neck, but I believed that was only to let me know the whole thing was working. I could barely hold my head up and Buddy had six heads as far as I could tell. He said my neck was much thicker than he could remember it being the day before. Miss Shady Lady would walk into the café any minute, crawl all over me, and kiss me with her pretty self.

"Billy, it looks like your eyes are about to pop out of your head."

"I'm fine, Buddy. You just wait until you see me strutting around with Miss Shady Lady on my arm. We'll see who the lucky man is then."

"You don't know anything about that lady. How do you know all that pepper and chicken feet business is going to work?" asked Buddy.

"Miss DuMont told me to wear this necklace, and Miss Shady Lady would be mine."

Buddy looked at me all quiet, and then he fell over the counter laughing. I could feel my head getting heavier and heavier, and the necklace getting tighter and tighter around my neck. Before I could say anything to shut Buddy up from laughing, I fell on the floor. All I could see was two sets of shoes, one a man's and the other was nobody but Miss Shady Lady's. Her little umbrella was beside those pretty little legs of hers.

"Billy, get up and stop playing opossum. We've got customers."

"Is he all right?" Miss Shady Lady asked. I tried to get up to see her face, but I couldn't move my neck.

"Yes, sir, what will you two be having today?" Buddy asked.

"Me and my wife would like your special."

"We don't have a special, sir."

Wife! What wife? I never saw a ring on Miss Shady Lady's finger. What was this crazy man talking about? Why was he coming into Madame's Café talking about "me and my wife"? If I could have gotten up, I would have knocked his head off his shoulders, grabbed Miss Shady Lady and rushed her down Main Street and on over to the courthouse so we could be married before this man started dropping lies on me again.

"I don't think he is all right. His neck is all fat and it looks like his head is about to explode," said that pretty voice.

"I think we better find us some other place to eat around here," said that lying man.

"Billy, you get up and stop playing opossum. He's just playing opossum, folks. He's not dying for real. Get up, Billy! Please stay, folks. What do you need? I can cook anything. Just name it. How about the best fried chicken you've ever tasted in your life?"

"No thank you."

I WOKE UP in Essie's house. She was holding a cold rag on my head. I had a cold rag on my neck too. It felt so good just laying there in bed feeling half asleep and half awake. Out of the cracks of my eyes, I could see Essie's face. She hummed.

"You feel any better, Billy? You've been sleeping for two whole days. You passed out down at the café and Buddy carried you all the way here. He told me you let Miss DuMont voodoo you."

I nodded.

"You don't have to talk at all. I understand. I know that you, garlic, peppers, and chicken feet don't get along. I told God I was not leaving your side until the old Billy came back. I prayed for you the whole time."

I grabbed Essie's hand. Those were the most beautifulliest words anybody had ever said to me. They sat in my head like a good dream. Essie didn't have as much fashion as Miss Shady Lady, and she didn't need to carry one of those little umbrellas around with her. She was just a good woman, plain and simple. I looked into those big eyes she had, and I could see all of our children, and me and her puffing on a cigar.

"I love you, Essie," I told her.

"That's just the fever got you talking like that, Billy."

"Will you marry me, Essie?"

Essie couldn't say one word. I saw the tears running down her face, then she hollered, "Yes!" She kissed me and her lips tasted like sugar cane. I sat up in the bed and held her. She was soft like a feather pillow. Her body was warm, and I knew she was warm inside, too, because she had the most kindest heart of any woman I had ever known. She prayed for God to bring me back to life when I was headed to the graveyard. I figured, if she would do that for me, she wouldn't mind being my wife and living with me for the rest of her life. And that's why I married Essie.

But that ain't the end of the story.

Miss DuMont came walking into the café after being gone for weeks. She said she had some bad news for us. She looked around to find something to complain about. When she couldn't find anything, she asked me for all the money we made while she was gone. I told her that it was the same amount she left us with before she went away. Then Buddy told her that I was a married man.

"See, didn't I tell you it would work, Billy! You listen to me. I will never lead you wrong."

"I'm not married to Miss Shady Lady. I married Essie."

"Who is that?"

"My new wife, that's who it is, and you ought to know what you're doing before you go around playing God."

"He was all stretched out on the floor, playing opossum. You should have seen him, Miss DuMont," said Buddy.

"Billy, you're what I call a bad chicken killer. But you're married now and that's all that really matters. Do you love her?"

"I do."

"Then that's all that really matters, good chicken killer or not. I've got something to tell the both of you. So listen good."

"What is it?" I asked.

"I got to go back down to New Orleans and see about some business. The government claims that I owe some back taxes. This place has to close down," she said.

"Don't close it down! Let us run it. Buddy and me got good heads for business when we put them together. Plus, he has been trying out some new recipes. That's why I can never keep all the dishes clean."

"What?"

Buddy just stood with his mouth open. He couldn't believe I was speaking up for him.

"You put his mind up to this, Buddy?"

"No, Miss DuMont. That's Billy's own mind working."

"Give us a chance, Miss DuMont. You'll come back here, and this will be a changed place."

She sat down and looked at the two of us. She tapped her heavy foot on the floor, then she took a minute to think.

"You'll need some extra help with me gone. We can't afford it right now."

"I can get Essie to help. She can take your place." Miss DuMont didn't do anything around the café anyway.

"Somebody will have to keep up with the money and the records. Buddy has the head for cooking. Who has the head for numbers?"

"Me! I've got a good head for numbers."

"Who's going to keep the place clean?"

"Me and Essie. We can clean and count at the same time."

"Buddy, what do you have to say about all this?"

"Give us a chance, that's all. If it doesn't work out, we can close the place down."

"All right, but I'll be back. If you two do anything crazy to my café, I'll have to put something on the two of you that will do worse than what was done to Billy."

"Everything will be just fine," said Buddy.

We hugged and kissed Miss DuMont. We couldn't pick her up and put her on our shoulders, because we would have fell into hell. I figured she probably knew the devil anyway.

I liked having Essie working with me at the café. She was getting a little fat in the stomach, but Buddy was cooking some of the best food the folks in Moon County had ever tasted. We had folks coming in all the way from Sparta County. I had to turn some folks away, especially Miss Shady Lady and her husband. Miss Shady Lady wasn't even pretty anymore, at least not as pretty as Essie. Some of the customers said she had a shine in her face.

Months later, I got a ladder and took down the Madame's Café sign and put up the new sign that said "Café." Buddy drove up in his new motorcar. He said Miss DuMont would probably voodoo all of us, if she ever came back to Moon County, but we hadn't heard anything from her. Essie was holding the baby, because I was a daddy. She said the sign was straight. We locked the doors to the café and Buddy gave us a ride to our new house.

Mattie

THAT BABY RAMUS was just as devilish as ever—kicking Dr. Pike in the shin and hiding under my bed with a jar of crickets. Dr. Pike drove all the way from Sparta County to check on me. He told me I was not allowed out of the bed. I had heard those same words a long time ago, when I fell on the floor in the kitchen and lost the baby. A smart man like Dr. Pike seldom minced words when it came to telling a woman like me the truth, especially when she had lost such a special part of herself. He let me rest all alone before coming into the room to whisper in my ear that there would be other chances. Why did I believe him? In those days, I believed in other chances, and I felt the door had not closed on me forever. After all, I was already a wife and a mother. There was cooking and cleaning. There was planting, picking, and milking. Porter and his daddy were always there, rising up between me and life and pushing out the fresh air and quiet. His daddy died when Porter was seventeen and I had grown used to Dr. Pike coming in and going out of our house and closing doors. I could see him when I closed my eyes to sleep and now his whispers were too loud. I laid in the bed listening to him in the other room, talking to Porter and Laura while he tended to Baby Ramus.

"Laura, Baby Ramus is fine, and a good spanking wouldn't hurt him none! He is running a little fever but catching crickets in a jar probably didn't cause it. If anything, he might be coming down with a September cold. You might want to keep him inside for a day of rest. And Porter, you shouldn't be making many plans that include old Miss Mattie. Let her die in peace. Nowadays, that's the best way."

Who was Dr. Pike calling old? There were days when I felt as young as I was when Porter was born. He talked as if somehow death had already met me walking along the road and would not let me pass. Laura was always there to comment, like what Dr. Pike couldn't tell Porter she could. Porter should have married a smarter woman. What made her ever believe that chicken soup could replace what seventy years of hard living took away from me? It never could. But Laura didn't believe much that didn't come from her own mouth—or Dr. Pike's. Her tongue was too quick and her ears closed. She was so hard to talk to because she didn't listen to me. There were times I had to remind her that Porter didn't listen to her, and she could never know a man like the back of her hand. She was a young mother with too much hair and pride. She hadn't lived long enough to know that, sometimes, the loved did not always love the lover.

"Baby Ramus, get down from there! If you don't get yourself down off that dresser, I'm going to have your daddy come in there and get up good! Don't let me catch you climbing on that dresser bothering those crickets again. Dr. Pike has already been out here once today. Get down from there before you wake up Miss Mattie. I told your daddy she wasn't well enough to keep good eyes on you. Sit in her rocking chair, like I told you. Get there! Right this instant!"

"Grandma Mattie is dead. I don't want to sit by her."

"No, she's not. Dr. Pike said she's just heavy sleeping. Now get down before I make your daddy take his belt off and come in that room and get you good. And you'd better not take off that sweater."

"Take a picture of me!"
"What?"
"Take a picture of me!"
"I don't have time to take a picture of you now. Didn't I tell you that I have to help your daddy out in the field? Now get in that rocking chair, right this instant."

"This morning, you said if I'm good you'll take a picture of me. I've been good too long."

"You haven't been good since the day you were born. Sit down in that rocking chair and don't let me peek through this window again and see you out of it or else your daddy is going to get you good."

Why did Laura like to waste time with such silliness? She thought she was a good mother because she said and did all the right things, but she didn't like washing the windows and scrubbing the kitchen floor. I told her that sometimes the windows and the floors were the only things a woman had to call her own.

Porter wouldn't have time to bother her about things like that. He always walked around the house looking worried. His daddy was like that. He worried about the payments he owed to Mr. Murphy over at the Moon County Bank. I worried that Porter would never learn to walk. I complained that the baby crawled for too long. He thought that was what all babies did. I stood Porter up, only to watch him fall heavy on the floor and cry. It was too much for a mother. I remembered those days of falling and crying and I realized that it was just too much for any mother. Dr. Pike came. Each time he told us that Porter was a child full of health. He should have given me some medicine to give to Porter. It would have put my mind at ease, and maybe I wouldn't have demanded so much from him. One of the ladies in the church told me that Porter had weak legs, and that I should rub a little cow manure on them and wrap them in wet cloth. Porter's daddy said that could never help Porter learn how to walk. But those were days when I had short patience and uneven love. Many days, I worked late into the quiet of the night. There were too many times when we'd both come in late from the field. Porter's daddy was either killing hogs or plowing the field. I remembered the day he walked into the kitchen with bloody hands and saw Porter spread across my lap with cloths wrapped around his legs. He watched me stare at the walls with my head held high. That evening, he sat Porter in a corner and walked to the other side of the kitchen. He pulled out a little toy. Porter rose on his own and walked across the kitchen floor to him. His daddy looked at me and told me that I was silly and foolish and that he did not want gravy on his chicken. We sat down at the kitchen table for another quiet supper.

"Baby Ramus, is Porter sitting at the kitchen table?"

"Grandma Mattie, breakfast is over and my momma said I was a good little boy because I ate all of my food."

"Go tell Porter it is time for dinner and his daddy wants him to get out of that corner and come sit at the table."

"My momma told me not to leave this room, and I ain't moving because she said she was going to take a picture of me."

"Baby Ramus, come hold Grandma Mattie's hands."

"No! I don't want to. I'm drawing a picture."

"Don't you want to hold Grandma Mattie's hands so they can stay warm?"

"No! You're going to pinch me."

"Grandma won't pinch you."

"I ain't moving. My momma said she was going to take a picture of me. If I move, she won't take it."

If Laura had listened to me, she never would have wasted so much time telling him lies. She would have known that truth was somewhere waiting for Baby Ramus. I wished I could sit her down at the kitchen table and make her do her homework all over again. I kept pencils in the kitchen drawer because Porter was always losing his. I walked in and saw him with his head down and papers and pencils were scattered all over the kitchen table. I put down my coat and the egg basket and sat there until he finished. Porter could not leave the table until he finished his homework. If I had known better, I might have been able to see then that this was the beginning of what the teachers at the schoolhouse would later call the "problem" with Porter. I wished there was some good woman somewhere who could have told me what it was all supposed to mean.

Would I have listened to her? I was pulled in so many directions with so many things to worry about. I was tired. I looked older than my years. I didn't want to add to the worries already sitting on my shoulders like heavy laundry baskets. School was such a small thing to worry about. Talk about teachers and books was such a small thing. There were too many long nights of fighting about small things. We were a family that was uncomfortable with one another's ways. We were all so stubborn in quiet ways. I let the small things be. There was always cotton to be picked. There were all those dead corn stalks that needed to be cut down. There was the constant weariness in my mind about frosts lasting until late March, and the sinking feeling I felt in my stomach when we explained to Mr. Murphy why our payments were late, again. I didn't see much use in arguing with a man who blamed me for doing nothing to stop Porter from burning the first book the teacher had ever given him. I believed that fire could make children good. Silly woman. Foolish woman. Later, I realized that pulling the pages out of a book and throwing them into a fire really couldn't make a child good at all.

"I'm hot!"

"Baby Ramus, you put that sweater back on!"

"I'm hot."

"You're not hot! Put that sweater back on or else I'm not going to take a picture of you."

"This morning, you said that if I'm good you'll take a picture of me, and I've been good all day, and the crickets in my jar don't sing anymore, and I'm tired of sitting in this rocking chair."

"Stop that crying before you wake Miss Mattie up."

"Grandma Mattie is dead! She won't say one word when I ask her something. I've been good too long. You said if I'm good you'll take a picture of me."

"Hush up with all that silly talk! Work on your letter printing."

"I don't want to work on letter printing. I hate letter printing."

"Draw then. Don't you want to be a artist when you grow up?"

"No, I want to be like Dr. Pike, so I can make Grandma Mattie talk to me."

"The only way you can be a doctor is if you stop crying and draw."

"Then you'll take a picture of me?"

"Yes."

She should have told him no. It would make things easier for him if he learned to trust that word sooner rather than later. It would help him to survive. Many children do not survive no matter how much the reverend's wife prays for them and begs them to give Easter speeches in church. The reverend's wife begged Porter to give his speech in front of all the church members. She handed him a piece of candy wrapped in foil paper and he said yes. His daddy thought a twelve-year-old boy was too old to give an Easter speech. He said there was not enough money to buy a new shirt for Porter after Mr. Murphy came to the house and told him that it did no good to keep explaining lies. He asked me why I didn't make Porter a shirt, like I had done so many times before. I told him I thought it would help if Porter was dressed like the other children. He said Porter was not like other children and that some people might not understand his ways. But I knew Dr. Pike would understand because he had a son about Porter's age. Dr. Pike told me his son had a closet full of new shirts. He gave Porter one of them to wear to church that Sunday. Dr. Pike told him everything would be fine.

Porter stood up in front of the congregation and opened his mouth, but nothing came out. He looked up toward the ceiling for the words to his speech, but they weren't there. He looked at the reverend's wife standing behind him. There was no candy wrapped in foil paper for her to give. Porter's daddy told me that Porter couldn't give an Easter speech in front of all of those staring eyes. Somehow, I convinced myself that Porter could. I prayed about it. I spent all of those late evenings at the kitchen table listening to him repeat the words like a song. That Sunday morning, he asked me if everything was going to be all right. I told him everything would be fine, not understanding how much it might cost me if I was wrong.

When the children laughed Porter out of the church, his daddy stood up because I couldn't. I watched all of those eyes turn towards him as if people expected him to give the speech for Porter. His daddy only apologized. I had no words. I just hoped God would make my punishment something I could bear. I hoped the good people in church knew that Porter wasn't the cause. I was. It was too late for me to explain everything, so I sat in silence. I was ashamed to admit that his daddy was right: Porter was different. He had probably run off to hide in some corner somewhere, recognizing for the first time in his life that some people weren't good at all and that there were no reasons left for him to trust me.

"Baby Ramus, are you being a good little boy, sitting in that rocking chair drawing a picture for your momma?"

"Are you and Daddy almost finished working?"

"Yes."

"I want to be a doctor when I grow up because I have been good since this morning and you're going to take a picture of me."

"I'll take it when we finish, and only if you are a good little boy."

"What if Grandma Mattie died before you finished?"

"Miss Mattie will not die before I finish. Dr. Pike said she has plenty of time to see you grow up. Put your pointing finger under her nose."

"I feel air!"

"See. What did I tell you? Miss Mattie is just heavy sleeping."

"I don't want to sit in that rocking chair anymore. I'm sleepy. Can I go to sleep in the bed, too?"

"Only if you are good and go straight to sleep just like Miss Mattie."

Just like Miss Mattie, Laura said. I was never the model. Was my experience of any use to her? I wished she would cut her hair and close her mouth. I wished that she would clean the windows and scrub the kitchen floor before she cooked the chicken. And no gravy. Porter will not eat gravy on his chicken and neither would his daddy. When his daddy died, Porter was seventeen years old and had run away from home more times than I care to recall. He left home with his books every morning, but he didn't go to school. I spent so many days at the sheriff's office trying to keep Porter from being sent to the reformatory. He missed too many days in school, so he had to repeat grade ten twice. Miss Watkins sat behind her desk full of papers. She held a folder in her hand that she said indicated that "Porter's ability to learn certain basic concepts was low." Miss Watkins never told me what those basic concepts were and why they were so important. I asked her if she knew anything about cotton fields, and she stared at me with suspicion. I asked her what she thought her momma might have lost raising her, and helping her daddy make a living when times were hard. She said my questions seemed "irrelevant to the conversation at hand, because the real problem was why Porter couldn't learn the basic concepts." I told her how Porter once nursed a cow back to health after infection took her down for two weeks. I told her how he could kill a hog and have the meat tied and hanging up in the smokehouse before dark. I asked her did she have a test that told her what those things might indicate about him. But she just looked at me like she was surprised I could even form the question. She never answered me.

Porter sat in a chair in the corner the whole time I talked to Miss Watkins. I called him over to her desk and asked him what he thought. Porter told me and Miss Watkins that he didn't see much use in school anymore, and he thought he was better at growing things. Miss Watkins told him she thought he was making a big mistake, and he would regret the day he ever left school. Porter spoke before I could. He told her she didn't know what he would regret, because she didn't know him. I reached out to him, but he pulled himself back as if the hand that tried to touch him would do more to hurt than help. Porter walked out of that classroom, and I knew that had changed him more than fire ever could. That day changed me. It was the day that the part of me that was a part of him died. I didn't need a folder full of indications, like Miss Watkins, to know that.

I told her God would help Porter. I told her that putting everything in the hands of God was the best way. One day, Laura will have to travel the same road with Baby Ramus. I hoped that she would be ready for the journey. The world had a different story to teach her and she would have a different story to tell. All of those years I fussed and fiddled and Laura never understood what kind of woman I was. I was a silly woman, a foolish woman, and a woman who killed a part of herself with her own hand. I believed in Dr. Pike. I believed in chances and whispers, and open doors. Why bother with memories that were precious yet unwanted? Maybe they mattered so much to me because they didn't matter at all to anyone else. Maybe the words Dr. Pike whispered in my ear just before he closed the door on me forever were too hard and too true for any woman to live by. People die, he said, regardless.

"Baby Ramus, you should be ashamed of yourself for doing that! Take every last one of those crickets off Miss Mattie's forehead and put them back in that jar. Right this instant!"

"They're dead."

"Why aren't you being a good little boy?"

"Because you're a liar. You're not going to take a picture of me and you know it!"

"You take back those words, or else I'm going to make your daddy send you to the reformatory. You take back those words right now, Baby Ramus!"

"No! You lied to me."

"Put those crickets in that jar. Right this instant! Here comes your daddy. He's going to get you good for being such a bad little boy."

"No, he's not!"

"You just wait and see. Your daddy's coming in there to get you good for being such a bad little boy and talking back to your momma."

"No, he's not because Grandma Mattie is dead."

"Hush, Baby Ramus! Bad little boys like you can't play doctor. Get that cricket off Miss Mattie's nose! She's not dead, so stop that playing and let her be."

"Well, how come I don't feel air, and I don't want to have my picture taken or be a doctor anymore?"

Abel

"Come on in and catch your breath, Jeeter. Dr. Randolph knows he was supposed to wait before he made that turn on Main Street. He almost ran you over."

"He see me just as clear as day," Jeeter said. "That rascal tried to run me over on purpose."

"You know, that's a new motorcar he's driving. He told me he just got it last Saturday." I brushed the last of Dr. Randolph's hair out of the chair so Jeeter could sit down.

"What he want for free this time? You know he always wanting something for nothing." Jeeter patted the sides of his head to let me know he just wanted his hair trimmed.

"He thought I should give him a free shave with his haircut. He's been coming to my barbershop for years. He knows a shave is going to cost him extra."

"He pay for it?" asked Jeeter.

"He takes out his wallet and tells me he didn't have any extra cash."

"That's a lie. Dr. Randolph keep money."

"Then he says he'll pay me extra the next time he comes in. The chances of that happening are about a million in one."

"Something just ain't right when a man can buy motorcars all day and won't pay for the cost of a shave."

"That's right! I have a notion to do like Elma says and charge him interest."

"How's Elma doing these days?"

"Not good. She cries about being a grandmomma. She thinks she's getting old."

Jeeter jumped like I poked him with the comb. "You never told me Dorthea be pregnant."

"Dorthea adopted some child from overseas. She did it all through the mail. She has to send money every month. Just imagine how you would feel if that was the first thing you heard in the morning?"

"Abel, that's crazy! Who ever heard of somebody adopting a child through the mail? I don't even think that's legal."

"I'm telling you, Jeeter. Dorthea had all kinds of papers, and they looked legal to me. She even had a picture of the child."

"What the child look like?"

"To tell the truth, the child looks just like Dorthea does now, with all of her hair chopped off. I mean, imagine what a little boy would look like standing next to a river; except he is really a little girl with sticks for arms and legs and a bubble belly."

"You mean the gal don't have any pigtails?" asked Jeeter.

"The only way that girl could get pigtails is if somebody drew them on that picture."

"All gals should have pigtails. I remember Dorthea use to have pigtails when she was coming up. Why she go and chop off all that good hair she had and put on overalls? She look peculiar now."

"I don't know what's gotten into Dorthea, but I do know that Elma's heart broke like glass when Dorthea walked through the door with all her hair gone, and she said she was free from centuries of oppression."

"What hair got to do with oppression?" asked Jeeter.

"I don't know, Jeeter. But guess who Elma blames for the whole thing?"

"You?"

"Me."

"Why she pin the blame on you?"

"I don't know. Sometimes, I think that Elma believes I'm the cause for everything Dorthea has done wrong with her life. She says I cursed the girl."

"You let Elma talk to you like that? I wish Lucille would talk to me like that."

"Elma pretty much says anything she wants to say. When she told me I cursed Dorthea, you know who that reminded me of?"

"Otis Butler!"

"Sure did, and that almost scared me to death! So I told Elma that Dorthea wasn't cursed, and that I was just making sure the girl at least knew how to run this barbershop. Who else did Elma think was going to run this place when I died? Dr. Randolph is going to ship Junior off to some school in Atlanta to learn how to pull teeth and run his practice. I think hair is just as important as teeth. So why can't I do something like that for Dorthea before I die?"

"There you go conjuring your own death again."

"I've been thinking about death since Elma told me that I cursed Dorthea. She thinks I put too many of my ways on her. She's too headstrong, Elma says. She says no man will ever want to marry a girl with a strong head."

"Elma might be right on that. Dorthea ain't like the other gals."

"You know what Dorthea did, don't you?"

"What?"

I stopped cutting and Jeeter turned around to look at me. "You mean I didn't tell you what Dorthea did?"

"No! You didn't tell me nothing. What she do?"

"Dorthea quit her job at the café, and signed herself up for a night school class with that new teacher from Atlanta that the school board just hired. What's his name?"

"Mr. Laclede!" said Jeeter.

"Yeah, that's him. Dorthea thinks she needs to relearn history."

"I bet Mr. Laclede can help her. I hear he a good teacher."

"That's what Dorthea said, but I can't figure how she can say the man is a good teacher if she ain't ever been his student," I said.

"Oh, you can tell he good. He ask all kinds of questions. His mind sharp as a knife. The other day, I went into the café and had a cup of coffee with him. I told him about how Bo drowned in the Oconee River, and how I've worked at the cotton mill for over twenty years. He thought that be the most interesting thing he ever heard."

"He did? What did he think was so interesting?"

"I guess all of it. I show him my cut marks from the machines. Then he ask me some more questions about my job and whether I be happy working there."

"Well, that sounds pretty much like the way he acted when he came in to get his first haircut. He asked me all kinds of questions about the barbershop business. I told him that Dorthea signed up for his night school class. He thought that was the best news he'd ever heard. He said he wanted to get more folks in the community involved in learning."

"That was the same thing he say to me."

"Well, he told me I should sign up for that class too. I thought about it, but what do I look like sitting up in the schoolhouse, as old as I am? I told him I once took a few of those correspondence courses. You should have seen how surprised he looked when I told him that."

"Does the child go to school?"

"Sure does. Dorthea says the child knows three languages. You'd never know that just by looking at that picture."

"I bet I would, if I saw what she look like."

"How, Jeeter?"

"It be in the eyes. The eyes tell the story. What's her name?"

"Whose name?"

"The adopted child."

"I don't know. I'm pretty sure Dorthea told me this morning. I'm sure I'd just mess it up if I could remember what it was."

"No, you won't. Just sound out the letters. And if that don't work, you can always give her a good old fashion American name. I bet she look like a Margaret."

Jeeter took his money out of his wallet. I could hear the door squeak as it opened. Ossie B walked in wearing dirty overalls with no shirt or shoes.

"Mr. Jeeter is rich! Mr. Jeeter, I bet you the richest man in the whole world. I bet you just sit at home all day and think about how rich you is."

"Ossie B, get out of here with that song and dance show. What have I told you about spying on my customers? I've told Rosetta a million times about you. I'm going to have the sheriff come and lock you up in the jailhouse."

"My momma say I can go wherever I want. I'm a man."

"Do your momma know you walking around here with no shoes on?" asked Jeeter.

"My momma say I don't have to wear shoes. I'm a man."

"You're not a man. Now get out of here with that foolishness before I have the sheriff come arrest you."

"My momma say a man can go wherever he want! You just mad because Mr. Jeeter is rich and you not. Everybody know barbers ain't rich."

"Ossie B, what have I told you about the words you let out of that mouth of yours? Haven't I told you that real men don't go around behaving like that," said Jeeter.

"How they behave then?"

"They behave like gentlemen. They don't go around bothering folks and they don't back talk they elders either," Jeeter said.

"Jeeter, what else do you expect to come out of that boy's mouth. No wonder everybody around here thinks he's cursed."

"What's cursed?"

"Something bad," said Jeeter.

"Mr. Jeeter, will you give me some money? Please, Mr. Jeeter. Please."

Jeeter reached into his pocket and pulled out his change. "You need to start acting better or the gals ain't going to like you none."

"I'm a man and I'm going to marry Dorthea!" Ossie B looked at me and smiled.

"That's a goddamn lie!" I yelled.

"I love Dorthea. My momma say a man is suppose to be in love."

"Abel, I'm surprise to hear you cuss. I can't even remember the last time I heard a cuss word come out of your mouth," said Jeeter.

"Dorthea is way too old for Ossie B. He ain't ever going to be fit for the future if you keep spoiling him with charity. Every penny he gets is wasted on ice cream cones over at that café."

"Abel, a little charity never hurt nobody. If Ossie B wasn't peculiar, he'd be just like Bo. My spare change never hurt Bo none."

"Well, I'd much rather Dorthea marry somebody like Bo than Ossie B. Just watch. He'll be just like his momma and never work a day in his life." Jeeter shrugged and walked out the door. He looked up at the sky. Just before the door closed, Ossie B turned around and stuck out his tongue.

"My momma say she don't have to work, because Grandpa Otis fought in the war and saved this country from the overseas people."

"COME ON IN, Mr. Laclede. Sit over there in a chair and make yourself at home. I'll be finished with Scout in a minute."

"Thank you, Mr. Bailey." Mr. Laclede crossed his legs and unfolded his newspaper.

"I told you that you can just call me Abel. You don't have to be so respectable all the time. Before you walked in, I was telling Scout here that one day I was going to get myself a new door for this old place. What do you think about that, Scout?"

"I think that would be nice, but it's going to cost you a lot of money. Gladys say inflation is going up again."

"Mr. Laclede, are you ready for Monday? That's when school starts, right?" I asked.

"Yes, and I'm almost ready. I went over to the high school this morning to start setting up my classroom. All the teachers met yesterday. They all seemed like nice people. In fact, I haven't met a mean person since I've been here."

"Just wait a while; this is Moon County," I said.

"Seriously, everybody is nice here. One of the teachers even invited my wife and me over for dinner."

"Who was it?" I asked.

"Mrs. Randolph."

"Get out of this world, Mr. Laclede. You mean you been over to Dr. Randolph house for a meal?" asked Scout.

"Yes sir."

"I don't know anybody around here who ever been over there for a meal. Do you, Abel?"

"Otis Butler said he went over there once."

"Get out of this world! I don't believe that and I don't believe Mr. Laclede was over there either. He probably never even made it past the gate. They always keep the gate locked."

"Well, the gate was opened for me already," said Mr. Laclede.

"Now, I know you lying. That gate is never open. I've thrown newspapers over that gate for years, and it always be locked. How come you get to walk through the gate and nobody else can?"

"Never mind Scout, Mr. Laclede."

"Never mind, my foot! Them folks think they kings and queens, and this ain't that kind of country. Ain't I'm right, Mr. Laclede?"

"That's what the history books say."

"Well, who cares what the history books say? Dr. Randolph owes me for a shave. Can you imagine a man with money not wanting to pay to get a shave, Mr. Laclede?"

"No sir, I can't say that I can."

"What was it like over there?" Scout tapped his foot against the chair.

"What was what like?" asked Mr. Laclede.

"Dr. Randolph house. What it like?"

"It was nice. Comfortable."

"I hear they got silk curtains on all the windows," Scout said.

"I can't say I really noticed the curtains."

"What they feed you? Steak, I bet," said Scout.

"We had chicken and green beans, and Mrs. Randolph made a sweet potato pie."

"Get out of this world! Mrs. Randolph can cook? Wait until I tell Gladys. Abel, I thought you said Dr. Randolph had a maid?"

"That's what Dr. Randolph told me."

"Did you see a maid, Mr. Laclede?" asked Scout.

"No, I didn't see a maid."

"Maybe, she be in the back or something. You know, not allowed to show up when the company over," said Scout.

"Well, that's hard to believe, knowing how Dr. Randolph likes to parade everything," I told him.

"What you all talk about?" asked Scout.

"Well, let's see. We talked about Junior going off to dental school in Atlanta. We talked about the new night school program at the high school. My wife and I talked about buying a house and starting a family."

"What's your wife name?" asked Scout.

"Catherine."

"That's a pretty name," said Scout.

"How come we haven't seen the two of you in church?" I asked him.

"My wife and I just haven't found the right church home."

"I bet you two Catholics, ain't you?" asked Scout.

"Yes, we are."

"I knew it," said Scout. "You look like a Catholic."

"Dr. Randolph suggested that we join his church."

"The church Dr. Randolph goes to is all the way in Sparta County, and it ain't Catholic. We have a perfectly good Baptist church right here in Moon County," I told him. "We take Catholics."

"We sure do. Benny wife use to be one," said Scout.

"Mr. Laclede, I'm inviting you to come visit our church. Services start tomorrow morning at eight o'clock sharp. You'll get a chance to meet my wife, Elma. She's dying to meet you. She's going to be a grandmomma."

"Congratulations."

"It ain't the way you think, Mr. Laclede. Dorthea went and adopted herself an overseas child through the mail. I ain't never heard of nothing like that before. Have you ever heard of such a thing, Mr. Laclede?" asked Scout.

"Yes, my wife's sister adopted a boy, but he didn't come from overseas."

"Where did he come from?" I asked.

"Shreveport, Louisiana. That's where my wife's sister lives."

"What did the boy look like?" I asked. I didn't look up, but I heard the door open and close.

"He was just a baby the last time I saw him. Now, I guess he might be the same age as that young man right there." Mr. Laclede pointed to Ossie B standing in the doorway with a pipe in his mouth.

"Ossie B, where did you get that smoking pipe?" I asked him.

"It's my Grandpa Otis pipe. My momma say I could have it. I'm a gentleman."

"Well, you look more like a fool to me," I told him.

"Miss Rosetta know better than that," Scout said. "Wait until I tell Gladys how she letting you run around with a pipe in your mouth. You'll be wanting tobacco next."

Ossie B strutted in front of us with his chest out; then he sat down in the chair next to Mr. Laclede and crossed his legs. "I know you."

"Who am I, young man?" asked Mr. Laclede.

"I'm a gentleman."

"Well, who am I, Mr. Gentleman?"

"Will you give me some money if I guess right?"

"Ossie B, what have I told you about pestering my customers for money?"

"It's okay, Mr. Abel. I don't mind."

"You that new school teacher, Mr. Laclede."

"That's right. You are smart, aren't you?"

"My momma say I am. But I bet I'm not smarter than you. I bet you the smartest man in the world. I bet all you do all day is sit around and be smart, don't you?" Mr. Laclede reached into his pocket and pulled out his change.

"That Ossie B sure try his best to have a silver tongue," Scout said.

"Mr. Laclede, don't you listen to Ossie B. He'll take every cent you gave him and go spend it on ice cream cones," I told him.

Ossie B stood by the door.

"Look at yourself in the mirror for a minute," I told him. "You're so busy trying to get to the café everyday you can't even make yourself look respectable. Your momma will have to take you to see Dr. Randolph if you keep eating ice cream cones."

"I'm not going to the dentist. My momma say I'm going to high school; then I'm going to college."

"Ossie B, you know you have to go to that special school out at the asylum," Scout said.

"My momma say it's a smart school because I'm smart. Go ask her."

"Nobody has to go ask your momma nothing," I told him.

"Then ask Dorthea. She give me extra ice cream when I count all the way to one hundred for her. I'm going to marry Dorthea. My momma say a man is suppose to be in love."

"That's a goddamn lie! I told you once that Dorthea's too old for you. Just because you can count doesn't mean you're smart," I told him. I brushed the hairs off Scout's face with the duster.

"Then ask me something smart. Just ask me."

"Okay, I'll ask you something smart," said Mr. Laclede. "How do you spell gentleman?"

"Everybody knows how to spell that word, Mr. Laclede. It's spelled g-i-n-t-a-m-i-n." Ossie B stuck the pipe in his mouth and ran across the street to the café.

"Well, Mr. Laclede, that's our future. That's what we all have to look forward to, a world full of peculiar children," said Scout after he handed me his money.

"I wonder what Otis Butler would say if he was here to see what a mess Rosetta has made raising his only grandchild. You're up next, Mr. Laclede. I'm done with Scout."

"Are you okay, Mr. Laclede?" asked Scout.

Mr. Laclede held his chin with his hand. "I'm fine. I'm just thinking about something."

"Don't let Ossie B get you worked up none. That's just how folks with slow minds act."

"But Ossie B's got potential. The right person could help him go a long way," said Mr. Laclede.

"Who? Ossie B?" I asked. "Ain't much help for him, Mr. Laclede. He's a half-wit, and he's going to be that way for the rest of his life."

"But, I see all that potential in him. Can't you see it, Mr. Scout?"

"No, I can't say that I see it, but Gladys tell me that I need spectacles."

"Can you see it?" asked Mr. Laclede.

"No, all I see is trouble. One day, that boy is going to get himself into something that Rosetta can't sweet talk him out of."

"Mr. Laclede, Ossie B is the way he is because he was born under a curse. It's not his fault though. His Grandpa Otis should get the blame. Ossie B will have to adopt a child like Dorthea, or he'll just pass that curse right on to the next generation of Butlers," said Scout.

"I don't believe that. That's just superstition," said Mr. Laclede.

"Mr. Laclede, I've been telling folks around here for years that Ossie B's not cursed. Do you think they listen to me?" I asked him.

"Gladys say Rosetta should have paid another woman to have Ossie B. That's what's coming here in the future. Gladys know all about it. She read about it in a magazine. She say they already doing it in Belgium. Don't that kind of knowledge make you just want to get out of this world, Mr. Laclede?" asked Scout.

"No, I think the more we know the better. Knowledge is the key to understanding."

I adjusted the chair after Mr. Laclede sat down and I pinned the cape on him.

"Well, I wish Dorthea would have kept some of her knowledge about this adopted child to herself until me and Elma have had time to understand it. I don't think Elma can accept this new overseas grandchild. It's like everything is turned upside down and inside out. Some days, I try to figure out when everything changed."

"I know when everything changed," said Scout, while he checked himself in the mirror. "It was when Mr. Ike Magnolia died. He be the one who changed everything around here."

"Who is Mr. Magnolia?" asked Mr. Laclede.

"Get out of this world! You mean to tell me you ain't heard about Mr. Magnolia?" asked Scout.

"No, sir, I haven't heard anything."

"You mean you went over to Dr. Randolph house for dinner, and he didn't mention one word about the murder?" asked Scout.

"Scout, you know Dr. Randolph wouldn't say nothing to him about that."

"How did Mr. Magnolia die?" asked Mr. Laclede.

"Somebody shot him," I told him.

"You better watch yourself around here, Mr. Laclede. The folks in Moon County might be nice, but they will put a bullet in your back before you can say Peach State," said Scout as he closed the door behind him.

"Come on in and sit down, Homer. I just started on Mr. Laclede. You can read that newspaper over there on the chair while you wait."

Homer picked up the newspaper and sat down. "Whose newspaper? I don't like messing with somebody else's belongings. That's how folks get shot around here."

"That's Mr. Laclede's newspaper. He doesn't mind if you read it while you wait—do you, Mr. Laclede?"

"No, help yourself and don't worry. I don't even know how to shoot a gun."

"What? You don't! Well, you just surprised the heck out of me. I ain't never met a man who didn't know how to shoot a gun. They didn't learn you how to shoot in the army?"

"No sir, I've never been in the army," said Mr. Laclede.

"Both my sons in the army. God bless their souls. It's the best school in the world. The army is learning them how to be men." Homer opened the newspaper then folded it to one side.

"The army drafted a lot of us around here for the first war. Most of us were even lucky enough to make it back home. Homer thinks everybody should go to the army."

"None of us knew a thing about the world until we went into the army. They run me and Otis Butler through training and right into battle. Otis got half his leg blown off," said Homer.

"I worked as a barber in the army. I didn't know the first thing about cutting hair until they taught me."

"What did the army do with Mr. Otis after he got hurt?" asked Mr. Laclede.

"Them doctors put him up in the hospital and fed him all the ice cream he could stand. Then they give him a wooden leg and learned him how to work on motorcars. Otis was crazy about motorcars," Homer said.

"And he was crazy about gin, too. Otis and Homer were the best motorcar mechanics in Moon County. Then Otis started drinking every day. He stopped speaking to Homer, because he said he stole business from him, but a lot of folks still took their motorcars to Otis," I told Mr. Laclede.

"Percy Randolph take all his motorcars to Otis for fixing. Percy wouldn't let anybody touch his motorcars except Otis. It was nothing to see Otis driving around in one," said Homer.

"If you'd been in the army, Homer and Otis would fix your motorcar for free. They'd consider you family," I told him.

"First, I'd have to buy a car. I like walking," said Mr. Laclede.

"We had to stop giving free service because we started to lose money. Then, Mary left Otis and all he did was drink gin and fuss about being broke all the time," Homer said.

Mr. Laclede asked, "Did Dr. Randolph fight in the war?"

"Heck no, Percy didn't fight," Homer said. "But he know a lot about guns though."

"And what's worse, he has the nerve to tell folks he didn't have to go fight! He was probably hiding in some school somewhere learning how to pull out a wisdom tooth."

"What's wrong with that?" Mr. Laclede leaned his head to the right, and I moved it back towards me so I could get a better view.

Homer said, "All of us should have went over to fight. What make Percy any different from anybody else? And guess who else didn't fight?"

"Who?" I asked.

"Ike Magnolia."

"What? Mr. Magnolia sat right here in this barbershop and told me he was a veteran."

"Well, he ain't no veteran in my book. I work on his brakes once, and I ask him. He say he glad he didn't fight in the war," said Homer. "He say he didn't understand what we were fighting for."

"I can't believe he said something like that, Homer."

"Is this the same Mr. Magnolia who was shot?" asked Mr. Laclede.

"How you know about Ike getting shot?" asked Homer.

"Scout brought it up right before you walked in," I told Homer.

"I wouldn't listen to Scout if I was you, Mr. Laclede. All he remember is what Gladys tell him to remember," said Homer.

"Well, Mr. Magnolia sat right in my chair and told me he fought in the war. I never saw him as the type of man who told lies."

"Everybody tell stretchers. Heck, that's all the folks do around here. I believe it's just the way human beings be made up," said Homer.

"I don't believe that," said Mr. Laclede.

"You mean you never told a stretcher before?" asked Homer

"That's not what I meant. I just always try to tell the truth. I don't believe that all folks tell lies," said Mr. Laclede.

"Well, they might not where you come from, but folks in Moon County tell stretchers all the time," Homer told him.

"You got that right. Dr. Randolph is one of the biggest liars I've ever seen in my life. He expects me to believe that he's going to pay me extra the next time he comes in. He is the biggest liar ever born."

"Heck no, Ike get the first place prize for that," said Homer. "I always called him Ike, Mr. Laclede. It ain't no disrespect though."

"What did he lie about?" I asked.

"For one, he went around saying that a spelling bee would be good for the school children and it end up not being good at all."

"Mrs. Randolph asked me if I'd be willing to serve on a committee to help bring back the spelling bee. She says it's been a long time since the school had one," said Mr. Laclede.

"I bet she don't tell you why the school board got rid of it in the first place," said Homer.

"Why did the school board get rid of it?" asked Mr. Laclede.

"They didn't have a choice, really," I said. "You see, the school board hired Mr. Magnolia to improve the high school down here the way he did up in Washington, D.C. Mr. Magnolia came from old money. Folks who come from old money think they know what's best for everybody. The folks in Moon County thought it wasn't right to have a man over the school who didn't have a wife and children of his own. Mr. Magnolia always said he was married to his job."

"Well, I say the man was peculiar. He had me believing a spelling bee was going to do some good around here, but neither one of my boys got called to be in it. The whole fuss made Hattie think our boys weren't smart. I told her our boys be plenty smart. Just look at how good they're doing in the army," Homer said.

"When Elma found out that Dorthea was in that spelling bee, she bragged for days about how smart Dorthea was. You'd think it was Easter, the way she made us spruce up just to go and sit in the school gym."

"I remember Otis come in drunk. He be the main one fussing over a front seat," said Homer. "The children line up like soldiers. Then Ike call out the first word. You remember the first word, Abel?" asked Homer.

"No, all I remember is that Mr. Magnolia called it out and every child on that stage got the word wrong."

"I wish you could have been there to see it for yourself. Ike call another word and not one child on that stage could spell it right."

"What did the people do?" asked Mr. Laclede.

"Well, Otis stand up and pitch the first fit. He say the whole thing was unfair, because the words were too hard," said Homer.

"Mr. Magnolia said he got those words from some national office in Washington, D.C.," I said.

"Then Joe stand up and tell Ike that he ain't in Washington, D.C., and that his boy be needing Georgia words. Everybody start shouting and clapping like Joe preaching a sermon. Then Benny get up and tell everybody that Ike be shaming the children in front of us on purpose."

I said to Mr. Laclede, "Otis called him a traitor and told him that they shot traitors in the army. Mr. Magnolia tried to explain that the spelling bee wasn't over and there was bound to be a word on the list that one of those children could spell."

"Then Otis call for Ike to get some Georgia words, and everybody start clapping and saying hallelujah. Ike say there ain't no such thing as Georgia words. Otis say Ike was trying to show off his fancy education because he thought he was better than us."

"I remember Mr. Magnolia left the stage, shaking his head. Then Dr. Randolph walked up on the stage and told everybody that all the children did a good job and he would clean their teeth for free if their mommas brought them to see him. Elma took Dorthea and Dr. Randolph found one problem after another. Dorthea's rotten teeth cost me a year's savings."

"What happened to Mr. Magnolia?" asked Mr. Laclede.

"You see, Joe ask everybody to sign a piece of paper calling for Ike to step down as the principal until he came up with a list of Georgia words, but Ike won't step down for nothing. The school board end up firing him, because folks threaten to stop sending their children to the schoolhouse. Then Otis shoot Ike and his family been cursed with bad luck ever since."

"Don't believe that, Mr. Laclede! Otis didn't shoot Mr. Magnolia—Dr. Randolph did. I've been telling Homer that for years."

"Abel, Percy not the one who killed Ike and you know it! Look at all the good luck Percy has had. All Otis got was a wooden leg. What kind of god hands a golden goose to a cold-bloodied killer?"

"Homer is like everybody else around here. Folks in Moon County don't like to hear the truth."

"I hear what you saying, Abel. I just don't believe you, because that ain't the way I remember things happening back then. Ike had to leave Moon County or Otis was going to make him leave, but Ike was one of the stubbornest men I'd ever seen."

"That still doesn't mean Otis did it. Plus, the two of you weren't even speaking to each other when all of this happened."

"That don't matter none. I still stand up for Otis that Sunday the sheriff come to the church service and ask us who did it. Otis say he did it; then Joe stand up and say he did it. Benny say he did it. Jeeter and Scout say they did it. When I see the way things going, I stand up and say that I did it, too. Percy be the last one out of all of us to stand up. The sheriff shake his head and say God would surely curse whoever killed a good man like Ike."

"Did you say you killed Mr. Magnolia too, Mr. Abel?" asked Mr. Laclede.

"Yes, I did."

"Why?" Mr. Laclede looked confused.

"I was a soldier, and I knew I had to live the rest of my life in Moon County with the rest of those crazy fools who stood up."

"What about you, Mr. Homer? Why did you do it?"

"I had to do it. I had to stand with the family. Good or bad, Otis was family. I'd known him all my life. I wasn't about to stand by and let him go rot over in the Sparta State Prison—not after what he did for this country in the war."

"That sounds like an excuse to me," said Mr. Laclede.

"You see, it ain't about excuses. It's about brotherhood. You don't turn on your brother," said Homer. "They learn us how to be brothers in the army."

"I stopped believing Otis killed Mr. Magnolia a long time ago, because Otis told me that he didn't do it, and I believed him."

"Why would Dr. Randolph kill a man who was trying to do so much for the people in the community? It just doesn't add up," said Mr. Laclede.

"Because Dr. Randolph has always been able to do anything he damn well pleases in Moon County!" I yelled. "Nobody ever said that what he did was supposed to add up."

"Heck, Abel, you don't have to get mad at the man for asking a question. He only cuss when he get mad, Mr. Laclede. It ain't no disrespect though," said Homer.

"That still sounds like a silly excuse to me. Nobody can just do anything he wants," said Mr. Laclede.

"Well, you're wrong because I'm telling you right now that Otis Butler sat in here and told me that Dr. Randolph killed

Mr. Magnolia. It could have been any one of us around here, but Mr. Magnolia was the one he picked to kill."

"What do you mean?" asked Homer.

"Otis said Dr. Randolph brought his motorcar over to get the engine checked and asked Otis what it felt like to kill a man in battle."

"He was probably remembering things wrong. Otis forgot a lot of things when he was drinking," said Homer.

"I don't remember Otis drinking that day. He said when Dr. Randolph asked him what it felt like to kill a man in battle, he told him that, after a while, he didn't feel nothing. Otis told me that killing got boring, just like any other job. He said after a while, you don't even have to think about what you have to do. You just do it," I said.

"Mr. Abel, are you expecting us to believe that Dr. Randolph killed an innocent man just because he wanted to know what it felt like to kill a human being?"

"No, Otis told me Dr. Randolph was jealous of Mr. Magnolia. Otis could never figure out why because both of them had money. Now, you don't have to believe that. I'm just telling you what Otis told me."

"I still say Otis killed Ike and I'll take that to my grave," said Homer.

"Homer, Otis didn't do it! Otis said Dr. Randolph gave him a whole bunch of money and told him he was going to kill Mr. Magnolia. It was supposed to be a joke, Otis said; a joke told over a bottle of gin. He said that he never took Dr. Randolph at his word."

"You mean he give him a whole bunch of money just for checking the engine? I don't believe that," said Homer.

"No, Homer, he gave Otis that money for his gun, a closed mouth, and Otis's connections to us. Otis said Dr. Randolph knew he couldn't kill Mr. Magnolia without us protecting him. He said there wasn't a thing wrong with Dr. Randolph's engine, because that motorcar was brand new."

"Whatever happened to the gun?" asked Homer.

"Otis told me he threw that gun into the Oconee River after Dr. Randolph gave it back to him," I said.

Mr. Laclede shook his head. "Something must be missing from the story. None of this makes enough sense for me to believe Dr. Randolph killed a man out of jealousy." As Mr. Laclede was paying me, I could see Ossie B across the street. Ossie B was dressed in an old war uniform that was too big for him. He waited for a motorcar to pass before he crossed.

"I never said it was supposed to make sense. I'm just telling you how things really happened."

"Don't let Abel fester you none, Mr. Laclede," Homer said. "Here come Ossie B right now. He all the evidence I need. Just look at him dressed up in one of Otis army uniforms. Rosetta know better than to let him put that on. That woman got her hands full with that boy."

"I bet she wished a thousand times she could lock him in the asylum," I said as Ossie B ran through the door, breathing hard.

"Do your momma know you in Otis war uniform?" asked Homer.

"She say I could have it. I'm a soldier! And I'm rich, too!"

"What do you mean you're rich?" I asked him.

"Dr. Randolph give me two dollars." Ossie B waved the money at me.

"Goddamn it! You mean to tell me that Dr. Randolph is giving out two dollar bills to half-wits and he didn't even want to pay me for a shave! Give it to me! That's my money!" I walked over to Ossie B, and snatched the money out of his hand and tucked it into my pocket. He grabbed my arm. Mr. Laclede pulled him off of me and held him.

"Give me back my money! You can't take my money. I'm a soldier. I worked for that money."

"That's my money! Dr. Randolph owes me for a shave and I'm going to get every penny he owes me."

"It's my money. I worked." Mr. Laclede held Ossie B while tears ran down his face.

"You didn't work. Why would somebody like you be working for a man like Dr. Randolph? You're too stupid to even know what work is," I said.

"I know what work is. I'm not stupid. I'm a soldier. Go ask Dr. Randolph. He paid me for working."

"For God's sake, Abel, get a hold of yourself. You a old man fighting a boy over two dollars. I ain't never seen you act like this before," said Homer.

Homer and Mr. Laclede stared at me. I felt a little embarrassed, so I threw one of the crumbled dollar bills on the floor. Mr. Laclede picked it up and handed it to Ossie B.

"Where the other one at? Dr. Randolph give me two dollars."

"Well, I'm keeping one for charity."

"That ain't fair. You can't take money I worked for. You can't do that!"

"Let it be, Ossie B. I'll give you another dollar. Let's go on over to the café and get ice cream cones," said Mr. Laclede. He looked at me and shook his head.

"I don't want no ice cream. I want my dollar back. I worked for that money." Ossie B stomped his feet on the floor.

"Well, if you worked for this money, then I want to know what you did before I give it back to you. That's only fair, ain't it, Homer?" I asked.

"That's right," said Homer. We watched the door almost close behind Ossie B; then Mr. Laclede turned around and caught it with his hand. Ossie B stood in front of him, wiping his eyes with his arms.

"All right, tell them what you did to earn that money, Ossie B," said Mr. Laclede as he cut his eyes at me.

"I stood on the corner and guarded Dr. Randolph new motorcar while he ran into the five-n-dime. When he came out, he paid me two dollars. He told me that I was a good soldier and that all I needed was a war and a gun. Now give me back my dollar."

"No, I'm not giving you nothing. That's not real work, that's charity, and it's high time somebody put an end to all these handouts you've been getting."

"You a liar!" Ossie B started crying and yelling. "Dr. Randolph paid me that money for being a soldier."

"Ossie B, Dr. Randolph doesn't know the first thing about being a soldier, so shut up and get out of my barbershop before I have the sheriff come arrest you."

"Come on, Ossie B. I better take you home. You don't want to end up in trouble over a dollar," said Mr. Laclede as he pulled Ossie B out of the barbershop by his arm.

"COME ON IN, Rayford. You just missed Homer. He said he was going fishing when he left here."

"Well, it's a good thing you still here. I thought you'd be closed by now. Me and Etta Mae have to drive to Atlanta tonight."

"Sit on down," I told him. "What are you driving to Atlanta for?" I put the cape around his neck.

"We've got to go pick up Etta Mae momma. She coming to stay two weeks with us. I sure do hate it."

"I bet you do. There ain't nothing worse than having your mother-in-law staying under the same roof with you. It gives me a headache just to think about Elma's momma, and she's dead. That woman never gave me a moment's peace when she was around."

"That's how Etta Mae momma be with me. It's always something. My hair need cutting. My fingernails too dirty. I work too hard at the cotton mill. I'm too quiet. I eat like a bird. It's always something."

"Well, you have my sympathies. If things get too bad, you can always come hang out at the barbershop with me. I'm not doing too much of nothing these days besides getting ready to die."

"You sick or something?" asked Rayford.

"No, I'm not sick. It's just something Elma said to me. It made me think death is coming right around the corner."

"What she say?"

"Elma said I cursed Dorthea."

"What got into Elma to make her say something like that?"

"I'm not sure, but I think it has something to do with Dorthea chopping off all of her hair and adopting some child from overseas."

"A who from where?" Rayford asked.

"Oh, you haven't heard. Dorthea went and adopted some child from overseas, and she has to send the child money every month. I'm surprised Elma hasn't told Etta Mae."

"Well, I'll be darn. I don't think I know what to say about something like that, Abel."

"Me either, Rayford. Elma thinks it's all my fault. She said I put too much of my ways on Dorthea. I thought I was helping Dorthea, but Elma makes me think maybe I've done more harm than good."

"Well, maybe you should do like I do with Correen." I turned Rayford's head to the side a little so that I could cut behind his ear.

"What's that?" I asked.

"Let her be."

"But that's doing nothing at all. I thought you were going to tell me something special to do," I told him.

"That is special. You got to realize that Dorthea ain't a little girl no more. She a grown woman, and grown folks do exactly what they want to do these days. When I realized that, I let Correen be. So if she want to drop out of school and become a loose woman, then that be on her."

"Well, get this, Rayford, Dorthea finished school years ago. Now she's going back, and she's taking Mr. Laclede's night school class. That girl keeps me twisted upside down and inside out."

"See, there you go again. You still think Dorthea a little girl. You got to let her go. She ain't your little girl no more. She a woman. She a grown woman with her own mind and her own ways," said Rayford. I stood there thinking; then I moved Rayford's head to the left to get a better view.

"When did you get so smart?" I asked.

"You just have to learn to think smart when it come to things like that."

"I hope one day I can be like you. I have to admit I worry about folks going around saying that me and Elma didn't raise Dorthea right."

"It sounds like this whole fuss you making is more about you than Dorthea," said Rayford.

"Now that's a goddamn lie, Rayford! All of this is about Dorthea."

"No, it ain't. You just too stubborn to fess up about it," said Rayford. "You know I've always said you were too bullheaded."

"Well, how would you feel if Correen chopped off all of her hair and started wearing overalls instead of dresses? How would you like it if she told you over breakfast one morning that she adopted some child from overseas, and you can barely remember the child's name, much less claim it as your own blood kin? And if that's not the whole cake with the icing, I have to watch that crazy Ossie B run in and out of here all day talking about wanting to marry my daughter. Dorthea deserves somebody a million times better than Ossie B."

"You should stop letting that boy bother you so much," said Rayford. "Look, here comes that new school teacher, Mr. Laclede." I stopped trimming Rayford's edges and turned toward the door. Mr. Laclede stood there with no expression on his face; then he walked into the barbershop and shut the door behind him.

"You leave something here?" I asked.

"How you doing?" asked Rayford. Rayford waved to Mr. Laclede, but Mr. Laclede kept staring at me.

"I came to bring you something, Mr. Abel." He reached into his pocket.

"What? You paid me just fine, remember? You don't owe me nothing," I told him.

"I'm giving you back the dollar you took from Ossie B." Mr. Laclede held the dollar out to me. It had blood on it. I stared at him.

"What happened? Why does the dollar have blood on it?" I asked.

"Did you kill somebody?" asked Rayford.

"No. I'm just giving Mr. Abel back his dollar. Ossie B won't be needing it anymore," said Mr. Laclede.

"What happened to Ossic B?" Rayford asked.

"Why don't you ask Mr. Abel? He knows a lot about the Butler family."

"Stop beating around the bush. Did Ossie B hurt Miss Rosetta?" asked Rayford.

"Ossie B didn't hurt Miss Rosetta. Ossie B is dead."

"What?" asked Rayford.

"That's not true! That can't be true. Ossie B was just in here. He was standing right there where you're standing," I said.

"Well, don't just stand there with a closed mouth, Mr. Laclede. Tell us what happened," said Rayford.

"It's a goddamn lie, Rayford. Mr. Laclede is not telling the truth. Ossie B was just here a minute ago. I saw him with my own eyes." I shook my head.

"It is true. I walked Ossie B home after we left the barbershop. He went into the house, and I sat on the porch talking to Miss Rosetta about letting me tutor Ossie B. Then we heard a gunshot. We found Ossie B up in the attic lying next to a trunk full of old army gear. The gun was still in his hand. He must have been playing with it, and it went off. Take your money, Mr. Abel. Don't you think you've earned it now?" asked Mr. Laclede holding out the dollar.

"Goddamn you, Mr. Laclede. Who do you think you are, coming into my barbershop and pinning that boy's death on me? You think you can just walk in here and treat me like a murderer? Well, you can't because all the fingers are pointing to Ossie B. Just you wait and see. The sheriff is going to add everything up and not one finger will be pointing at me."

"Things will never add up for me," said Mr. Laclede.

"Well, they will for the sheriff and that's all that matters. Rosetta should have known better than to have a gun in the house with a half-wit. She should have never bought a gun in the first place," I said.

"She didn't buy a gun," said Mr. Laclede.

I stared at him for a while.

"Where did she get it?" asked Rayford.

"She told me that her daddy left it to her when he died," said Mr. Laclede.

"That's a goddamn lie. Otis Butler sat right here in this chair and told me he threw his gun into the Oconee River. Otis didn't leave no gun to Rosetta, and she knows it. Rosetta bought that gun."

"Well, it don't matter how she got it. Ossie B dead now and I hope Rosetta learning her lesson," said Rayford.

"She's learning more lessons than any of us will ever know, Mr. Rayford. I've learned something too. You want to know what I've learned, Mr. Abel?" Mr. Laclede walked over and dropped the dollar next to my foot.

"Don't be playing school teacher with me. I don't care what you've learned, and I'm sure as hell not going to let you stand there and pin murder on me. I'm not a murderer."

"I learned that Ossie B wasn't stupid at all. In fact, he was probably the smartest man I've met in Moon County." Mr. Laclede dropped his head and grabbed the knob of the door. "And you know what else, Mr. Abel? First thing Monday morning, I'm going to tell all of my students what a smart man Ossie B was."

"Well, you can tell the whole goddamn state of Georgia for all I care! Ossie B wasn't smart. He was a goddamn stupid half-wit who should never have been anywhere near a gun. Nobody around here is going to believe what you have to say about Ossie B."

Mr. Laclede shook his head and walked out of the door. I kicked the dollar away from me, hoping it would follow him.

"Well, Abel, I guess it's true what they say about those Butlers after all," said Rayford. "They are cursed."

"Shut up, Rayford. You don't know nothing about a curse. You're not that smart."

Rachel

I won't dance with no peckerhead, and that Frazier boy ain't nothing but a peckerhead. Mrs. Beckham been singing his praises every since he built that gazebo in her backyard, but he don't know what I know about Mrs. Beckham. She try to cheat folks out of their pay. That Frazier boy let her do just that to him. I overhear Mrs. Beckham talking fancy to her friends about how she got that gazebo built for almost nothing. If that Frazier boy ain't smart enough to know when he being cheated, then that ain't nobody fault but his own. He come over to my house and ask me out to the dance hall, and I say no. He told Mrs. Beckham about it, and she ask me why I won't go to the dance hall with him. I tell her right then and there that my daddy warned me about them peckerheads a long time ago, and I won't go nowhere with them, and I surely won't dance with them. Mrs. Beckham say I tickle her with my sass, but she not tickled one bit when I tell her that I won't be doing her laundry no more.

The word got out real quick about our spat. Mrs. Beckham told a whole bunch of lies about me. Now ladies hold up their hands and whisper when they see me coming. Some turn up their noses at me. Sometimes, two or three of the younger ladies stop me. They want to know if I'm as terrible as their mommas say I am. I tell them that I ain't no loose woman, and that I don't pray to witches at night either. Sometimes, folks in Moon County make up lies about things they don't even know about.

 I quit Mrs. Beckham on a Tuesday. I remember it like it was yesterday. I was standing in the kitchen ironing one of her blouses. My best girl, Sofia, usually come over to help me around eight in the morning. Sofia ain't much bigger than a line of wire, and she wear head scarves, cause she ain't much for fixing hair. Most times, she come through the door carrying Mrs. Murphy baby on her hip. The baby name Pauline, but we call her Pollie for short. Mrs. Murphy love putting Pollie in bonnets. I make Sofia take them off, cause it's just too hot to have a baby head all covered up in the summer heat. If she don't do nothing else, Sofia sure keep good eyes on Pollie while she working. Usually, I do the ironing and Sofia do the washing.

 Most of the time, we do more talking than anything. Sofia never run out of good things to say about them Murphys, mostly cause all of their old stuff end up being her new stuff. Mr. Murphy make loans at the Moon County Bank, and Mrs. Murphy don't do nothing at all. Anybody who listen to Sofia would have to wonder just what Mrs. Murphy doing four days out of a week that she can't keep Pollie. Sofia never ask her, cause she just crazy about Pollie. She even show me pictures of them Murphys holding Pollie in front of that vacation home they own over on Cherokee Island. In one picture, they huddled together with Mr. Murphy holding Pollie in the middle. Mr. Murphy in spectacles and shorts, and Mrs. Murphy in pearls with a puffy hairdo. Both of them got these wide smiles. They look like they living high on the hog to me. I ask Sofia how it make her feel when she look at that picture; then Pollie start her yapping like it's the second coming of Christ. Sofia pull her hands out of the washtub and wipe them on her dress. She walk over and grab Pollie off the pallet on the floor. Then Sofia turn around with a grin on her face and say the picture don't make her feel nothing except love for Pollie. I ask her if she ever feel like maybe Mrs. Murphy getting more than her fair share of the pie without earning it, and all we get is the crumbs left in the pan, and sometimes not even that. Sofia shrug her shoulders and say her boyfriend Sugar told her that some folks just luckier than others.

When Sofia bring up Sugar name, I want to scream, cause he ain't nothing but a peckerhead. Sofia work like a dog all day while he sit around drinking homemade gin like it's water. He can't keep a job longer than three hours. Sofia take any piece of job she can get and keep singing Sugar praises in the meantime. She let him sweet talk her into moving in with him. Sugar tell her he going to marry her and buy her a house on Cherokee Island. I tell Sofia she better stop letting that peckerhead fill her mind with lies, but it's just a waste of words. After two years, Sofia still shacked up with Sugar, and she still making the rent. The only person I ever hear mentioning anything about a wedding dress be me. I tell Sofia that Sugar just using her and stringing her along on a bunch of empty dreams. She just stand over the washtub hiding her smile behind her hand like she always do when I get her backed into a corner about Sugar.

That morning, I tell her to forget Sugar for a minute and think about herself. After all, we ain't getting any younger sitting around the kitchen doing other folk laundry all day. We still have so much life to live. I tell her we could even get ourselves a piece of that pie if we put our minds on it. Sofia just sit at the kitchen table gooing at Pollie and lifting her up in the air. Then she say Sugar told her I had more luck than most people, cause my daddy left me a house after he died. I notice Sofia raise her voice a little when she say that. I can't say nothing back, cause Pollie start yapping like it's the second coming of Christ, and she won't hush. Sofia pass her to me and I try to iron while I hold her with one arm. She start fussing even more and I pass her back to Sofia.

When I look up from my ironing, I see one of Sofia arms stirring in the washtub while the other one wrapped around Pollie.

She start singing "Ring around the rosie" and Pollie just eat that song up. She crazy about some "Ring around the rosie." I start complaining, cause the song sound like fingernails moving across sandpaper when Sofia sing it. Out of all the songs in the world, that be the one song that pipe Pollie down. I load up the basket, and I walk out the door with Mrs. Beckham laundry and let Sofia have as much of Pollie as she could stand.

I can't get to Mrs. Beckham house in one piece without them peckerheads coming after me. Joe John pop out of nowhere and scare me half to death. He take his hat off and bow. Sweat drop off his face like rain. I can tell he been drinking too much of that homemade gin. I tell him he need to go find himself a good place to rest, but he say that his sister won't let him in her house when he drinking. He ask me if I want any company on my trip to Mrs. Beckham house. I tell him no. Then he want to carry the basket, knowing he too full of gin to walk a straight line. I ignore Joe John and I carry my own basket.

Just when I get a little farther down the road, another peckerhead after me. This time it be Brady. He walk up to me dressed in dirty overalls. Brady carry a big box on his shoulder. He put the box down and take off his cap and kiss my hand. Brady a tall hefty man, and his voice make me think somebody pounding the drum in my ear. I ask him what the cardboard box for. Brady tell me that he going to sleep on it. I ask him how in the world he going to sleep on a box. He say he cut out the seams and spread it out under a tree. He told me it be real useful if you don't have any blankets around. Brady ask me if I need any yard work done around my house. He say he won't charge me one penny. I tell him that I do my own yard work. Then he tell me how pretty I look, and that he never seen a prettier woman in all of Moon County. I tell him he the biggest natural born liar I've ever seen in my life, cause I looked a mess. My hair be everywhere it ain't suppose to be and my dress full of sweat spots.

When I walk around to the back door, I see Mrs. Beckham sitting out in that gazebo talking. I can't tell who she talking to.

As I walk closer to the gazebo, I see exactly who Mrs. Beckham laughing and having a grand time with. It's Mrs. Murphy in pearls with a puffy hairdo. I look dead into Mrs. Murphy eyes as she pick up one of them cookies off the tray. All I can think about is Sofia, Pollie, and that washtub. Mrs. Beckham say hello to me like I'm the guest she not expecting. I drop Mrs. Beckham laundry in front of her. She scream for Grace, her maid. Grace come running out of the house like the gazebo on fire. Mrs. Beckham tell Grace to go get her purse. Grace turn around and head back toward the house; then Mrs. Beckham call her back and want her to come get the pot so she can bring back more tea. Grace get to the porch steps. Mrs. Murphy open her mouth and have Grace come all the way back to the gazebo again to get the whole tray so she can bring more cookies. It take everything in me not to scream.

Finally, Grace bring back the purse and Mrs. Beckham pay me. I check every penny real good. Mrs. Murphy tell me to tell Sofia she going to be picking Pollie up a little late that evening. My face get hot like metal when it's been sitting in the fire too long. The look I give Mrs. Murphy would have cut her if she moved an inch to the right. It take the spirit of Christ to keep me from rattling off a list of all the places Mrs. Murphy could go and how she could get there, but something else come out of my mouth that Tuesday. I know I spoke out of spite more than pride. I tell Mrs. Beckham that I quit and I won't be doing her laundry no more. You should have seen how she looked at me.

She ask me why. I tell her it's time for me to get out of the laundry business and move on out into life. Mrs. Beckham cover her mouth with her hands. Mrs. Murphy just snicker. I want to slap her. She had a whole lot of nerve sitting up in that gazebo drinking tea and eating cookies, while her own child was driving somebody else up the walls. She can make a fool out of Sofia if she want to, but not me. I'd drown myself in the Oconee River before I allowed that to happen.

I walk back home trying to figure out what I was going to do with myself. I run into them two peckerheads on the way, and something make me think about them in a different way. It's like the heat was spinning my mind. It dawn on me that there ain't but a few things really wrong with them. They still peckerheads, but ain't nobody said they had to stay peckerheads forever. The right woman could get the wrong man on the right track if she put her mind on it.

When I run into Brady, he still messing around with that box. I ask him how long it's been since he had a bed to rest in. He say he can't remember. I tell him to follow me. I lock my little arm with his big arm, and his eyes almost pop out of his head. We come up on Joe John sitting under a tree with a gin jar, and he grunt and frown. I tell him that it ain't what he think between me and Brady, and he goose up a little. I ask him how long it's been since he had a home-cooked meal. He say his sister let him come to dinner at her house, but only if he can keep sober. I tell him to put down that gin jar and follow me. I grab Joe John hand and his smile show all of his front teeth. I smile, too, cause I picture a whole bunch of better days ahead.

I rent rooms in my house to both of them. We sit down at the kitchen table every night for home-cooked meals. After that, we all sit on the porch and drink lemonade. Sometimes, Joe John mix his with a little gin, which is fine by me. He cut back long enough to get himself a job at Deacon Parker gas station. Brady already had him a few jobs lined up doing yard work. I eventually get both of them to clean themselves up real good, and go up on Main Street and buy some new clothes. My daddy always said, if you want to make a man feel brand new, just give him some soap and water and a place to call home, and that's just what I did.

We got along real good. Joe John and Brady go to work each morning after breakfast, and I spend most of my day doing whatever I darn well please just like Mrs. Murphy and Mrs. Beckham. I even have the nerve to have afternoon tea and cookies. You ought to see how I be lounging in the same kitchen where I use to crack my back over an ironing board. I still do laundry, but it for Joe John, Brady, and myself. It don't seem like work at all to me. My daddy always said you got to work hard to give what you want to get back. Something about that saying make real good head sense to me.

A few folks in Moon County don't agree. They start saying I run a harlot house. The reverend condemn Joe John and Brady to hell, and I'm the one leading the way. Sofia be the one person who I think know me well enough not to believe any of the lies put out against me. I think, out of everybody, she be the one to agree there ain't nothing wrong with a woman shacking with two men. After all, she was shacking with one of the worse peckerheads that ever lived.

One day, Sofia come over carrying Pollie on her hip and I tell her about my plan. I tell her that we never have to worry about doing laundry again. Sofia scream at me like she never done before. "What we?" she ask. "You mean you," she say. She accuse me of putting on airs in front of Mrs. Beckham and Mrs. Murphy. That ain't all. Sofia say that I invite two peckerheads I hardly know to live with me and I never invite her. She tell me she wouldn't have moved in with Sugar before marriage if I had asked her to move in with me first, but Sofia never ask me nothing like that. She say that if I was truly her friend, she shouldn't have had to ask me nothing. I apologize, but she don't accept it. Sofia say I don't mean it.

She tear into me real good that day, and it leave me feeling pretty down. I might not have had to take in laundry for a living no more, but I forgot that Sofia still had to. She say she wasn't lucky enough to be a woman every man in Moon County would be willing to pay top dollar for. Sofia know good and well I ain't that kind of woman. The relationship I had with Joe John and Brady be strictly about business. Sofia say she never know a relationship between a man and a woman to be strictly about business. I tell her that maybe she would if she stopped listening to that peckerhead Sugar all the time. I don't think she hear me cause Pollie start yapping like it's the second coming of

Christ, and Sofia start singing "Ring around the rosie" at the top of her lungs. Pollie pipe down long enough for me to hear Sofia announce that she and Sugar getting married. I tell her how happy I am and she roll her eyes. I start talking about being her maid of honor and making the cake. She tell me I ain't invited to her wedding. She say Sugar think it ain't a good idea to have me in it. He say it's too much of a stir up in the county about the way I live my life. I try to tell Sofia that she shouldn't let some peckerhead come between us on the most important day of her life, but she just walk out of the door crying and holding Pollie head against her chest. I stand in the kitchen wondering who come up with all them crazy rules on how to live life, and why I had to follow them. Then all of a sudden, I feel lonely and scared inside the way a woman does when there ain't nothing left at the party but her and the punch bowl, and I cry. I cry, cause I feel happy for my best girl, but I'm losing her all at the same time, and it hurt worse than flames on the skin. I be too scared to close my eyes, cause I don't want to see Sugar and Sofia in front of the reverend and Joe John and Brady in front of me. All I can hear in my head is Pollie yapping like it's the second coming of Christ and Sofia singing that song:
    Ring around the rosie
    A pocket full of posies
    Ashes, ashes
    We all fall down
 I'm sitting on the porch steps in tears when Joe John and Brady walk up to me. They ask me what wrong. I give them the long sad story and before I can finish, Joe John interrupt. He say he ain't going to rent a room no more. "Why?" I ask. He say it's cause of all the lies folks put out about me, and all the stares he get at the gas station. Some of the customers don't want Joe John to service them. Joe John say his sister told him that Deacon Parker said he might fire him if he didn't change his ungodly ways. I don't think that's right, cause I can't figure out for the life of me what God had to do with pumping crude. Joe

John reach into his pocket and hand me his rent money. I check every penny of it. He tell me he sorry and he need his job more than he need clean bed sheets and home-cooked meals. I tell him I understand. Joe John shake Brady hand and I watch him walk away.

    I look at Brady and the wide smile he got on his face. I ask him if he going to leave too. He say no, and that he going to stick things out with me even if he lost every job he got. I ask him if he believed any of them mean things folks been saying about me. He say that even if all of them things was true, he still wouldn't believe them. I have to catch my breath, cause them just ain't the kind of words you expect to hear from a peckerhead. You hear words like that from a friend. I ask him what he think about Sofia. After all, she still my best girl. Brady pull me closer with his big arm. He tell me that all good things happen in due time, and that Sofia would come around just as soon as all the noise about me quiet down.

    So I wait. Me and Brady dress up and go down to the dance hall. We fish in the Oconee River. We take long walks down back roads, and we sit on the porch at night and look at the stars. We make love, too, and we lay in the bed and talk until sleep decide to come. Brady ask me if I thought there would come a day when I'd want to get married. I tell him that I was in no rush to be a wife. I ask him why he never marry and he say he was never in no rush to be a husband. I think that be a real good answer, cause I don't want him getting any ideas about making an honest woman out of me, especially when things were going along just fine the way they were.

    But, I did miss Sofia. Weeks pass by and I get tired of waiting for her to show up at my door, so I show up at hers. I knock and she tell me to come in. Sofia ironing. I look around the kitchen. I see Sugar shoes in the corner and piles of laundry around the washtub. There ain't no trace of Pollie anywhere. Sofia say she started doing a lot of thinking about Mrs. Murphy after we had our spat. She stop babysitting Pollie for Mrs. Murphy, and she stop helping Mrs. Beckham with her laundry. Sofia tell me that she got herself a new job working as a maid for Mrs. Wick.

    She tell me something else that day too. She didn't get married. I stare at her like she was speaking in tongues. She say Sugar didn't ask her to marry him at all. She say that she lied to me out of spite more than pride. For a while, I don't know what to say to her. I just look at Sofia. I try my best to hold back my tears. I think to myself that maybe it's best I don't say nothing at all. I take a deep breath and stare at Mrs. Wick bed sheets soaking in the washtub. It'll take Sofia all day to finish them. I stand there in front of her, feeling like the only canary to make it out of the coal mine. I pull a chair over to the washtub and start washing the sheets. Sofia look at me. She hide her smile behind her hand. She'll be hiding that smile for the rest of her life, I think, and the tears start rolling down my face.

Earl

WE DON'T HAVE long-car caboose racing in Moon County anymore; it ended a while back. I was standing right there in Big Chaney and Little Chaney's hardware store the day it happened. I was measuring rope on the third aisle when Sheriff Espy and his men marched into the store and rounded the two of them up like cattle. The sheriffs kicked down the door to the backroom where Little Chaney sold his homemade gin; then they stomped out with a stack of cash, jars of gin, and the big chalkboard Big Chaney used to register all the runners and tally up the bets on the long-car caboose race. Sheriff Espy took the baseball bat that Little Chaney used to hit Sutter Jefferson on the head. He took all of the guns, including the pistol Big Chaney fired to start the caboose race. Old Judge Delahunt sent them both to the Sparta State Prison for racketeering. The whole thing scared folks in Moon County so bad that nobody even wanted to talk about long-car caboose racing, but Jesse did.

Jesse said locking up Big Chaney and Little Chaney had more to do with the county getting its hands on their cow pasture so it could be sold to some businessman who wanted to build a carpet factory close to the train track. The track curved into the pasture from the east and ran all the way to Atlanta. The two o'clock train that came on Saturdays always had the long caboose, and this was the one used for the race. Little Chaney lined the runners up beside the track and made sure they pinned their numbers on. When Big Chaney thought that the caboose was far enough ahead, he fired the pistol and the race was on.

Everybody waited at the top of the hill to see if the man who caught the caboose was brave enough to jump into the Oconee River before the train crossed the bridge into Sparta County. The man who made it back to the starting line first won the prize money, but he had to be able to swim the currents. Thunderbird Eddie was one of the fastest men around for years, but one year he wasn't able to swim the currents. We buried him near the long wire fence that separated the two graveyards. Then Lightfoot Leo started winning all the races. The man ran every race with bare feet until his leg got stuck in the caboose door when he tried to jump into the river. The train dragged him to his death. We ended up burying Thunderbird Eddie next to Lightfoot Leo.

Then Cluke had to go and get himself drowned in the river, and I had him buried next to our momma and daddy. Cluke loved the long-car caboose race more than any runner I knew. Cluke loved running so much he ran away from home ever chance he could get.

One time, I had to search all over Moon County for him. It was even harder trying to find him when Jesse wasn't around to help me. Old Judge Delahunt finally told me that if I didn't keep good eyes on Cluke, he was going to send him back to the asylum. Anytime Cluke ran away, I knew I had to go out and find him quick or there would be trouble.

Mostly, he liked to go out to the cow pasture and run along the tracks, or he'd go sit on the bank and throw rocks in the river. That morning, I walked down Main Street towards the river. I called Cluke's name, but the only thing that came to me was my own voice. I walked past the cow pasture and deep into the backwoods. I saw Cluke standing right in the middle of a field of grass. When I walked up to him, I noticed he didn't have any shoes on. His feet were bleeding and tears were in his eyes.

"Cluke, what's wrong?" He didn't say one word. "You know I've been looking all over for you." I expected him to say something. He grabbed my hand and pulled me along. "Cluke, where are you taking me? We need to get home while it's still daylight." He kept pulling me along, telling me he saw a dead dog. Nobody but a person like him would want to take the time to look at a dead dog. He pulled me along until we got over by the brush. There it was. I saw it with my own eyes, a human skull.

I told Jesse the next day. He didn't believe me. He said the older I got the more I acted like Cluke. I told Jesse I thought the skull we saw in the woods might belong to one of those missing boys we used to hear about on the radio news. Jesse said it wasn't worth reporting to Sheriff Espy because the person was already dead.

On the day before the last caboose race, I told Cluke to take my pocket watch out of his mouth so I could see just how late Jesse was. It was noon sharp and Jesse was nowhere in sight. Jesse used all kinds of excuses for not showing up when it was time to take Cluke out and let him run free. I saw Jesse hurrying down the road. Cluke waved at him. Jesse didn't bother coming up to the porch. He bent over on his knees and lifted his chest like he was going to blow the words out of his mouth with his breath.

"Come on, Earl," Jesse said. "Hurry up."

"What's wrong?" I asked.

"Sutter Jefferson is trying to sign up for the caboose race and Big Chaney won't let him. Little Chaney's got the baseball bat and folks are starting to place bets on Sutter's life!"

I straightened my hat and tightened the rope around Cluke's waist. The smell of trouble was always in the air any time one of those Chaneys got worked up.

"We ain't going to make it in time, Jesse!" I said.
"If Cluke hurries, we will. Pull!"
"Sutter's going to fly away to heaven like the fox and the rabbit, and they'll be eating sweet potato pie without napkins," said Cluke.
"Shut up, Cluke. We ain't got time for that foolishness today," Jesse said.
"Don't holler at him. It ain't his fault this is happening."
"I just don't understand why he always has to sing that stupid song when it doesn't make any sense. Nothing he says ever makes any sense. Shut up, Cluke!"
"Just pull, Jesse. Fussing at Cluke ain't going to change anything. You'll just make him nervous, and he'll have a conniption and wet his pants."
"I don't care. We have to get to Main Street and save Sutter," Jesse said.

SUTTER ALWAYS used to run up and down Main Street when he worked as a messenger for Old Judge Delahunt. When Sheriff Espy wasn't patrolling, a few of us used to sit on the courthouse steps and make bets on how fast Sutter could get a message from one place to another. Sutter wasn't even out of the courthouse doors good before somebody would ask, "Where're you going, Sutter?" He'd tell us and we'd place bets on a time using my pocket watch. Jesse won more bets than me because he knew before anyone else that Sutter liked to stop and sweet talk Sara. The last time we saw Sutter come out of that courthouse, he came out married to her. Then Old Judge Delahunt let Sutter go because he said he didn't have much need for a messenger anymore. All me and Jesse had left to bet on were the caboose races.

Not long after the marriage, Sara died of the cough. Nobody saw much of Sutter after that happened. Jesse said he never answered the door when he went to his house to check on him. He asked me if I had heard anything about how Sutter was holding up. I told him I hadn't seen or heard anything about Sutter since Sara died.

Cluke told us he knew exactly where Sutter was; then he started singing a song about Sutter flying away to heaven with a fox and a rabbit. Old Judge Delahunt said Sutter couldn't get a job driving the ice truck, so he took a job working on Jack Moffett's farm near Sparta County.

Early one morning, I tied the rope around Cluke, and me and Jesse put on our hats and walked out to the Moffett farm. When we got there, Mr. Moffett said he wouldn't tell us what happened to Sutter until we helped him move ten sacks of planting seed to the barn. I told Jesse that Cluke couldn't do work like that, but Jesse said the two of us would have to do it if we were ever going to find out about Sutter. I told Jesse the whole thing smelled like a skunk to me. Jesse said I was acting like Cluke again. I made Cluke sit with his back against the tree that stood next to the barn. Jesse tied the rope around Cluke and knotted it real tight. Cluke didn't even cry.

Me and Jesse almost threw out our backs for Mr. Moffett, only to hear him go on and on about how Sutter was a good worker until he disrespected him by accusing him of lying about his pay. Mr. Moffett said he always gave Sutter his fair pay, and he'd never cheat a man out of a day's pay when he knew he had a sick wife at home. Me and Jesse didn't say one word after Mr. Moffett said that. Cluke didn't say anything either. I asked him why he was so quiet and he said the tree was talking to him. Jesse told him to stop telling lies. Cluke said the tree told him that the fox and the rabbit were friends, but the rabbit jumped out while the fox stayed in. He said he wanted to eat sweet potato pie and rabbit for dinner. Jesse threw his arms up and let out a long breath. He said he would hold his hands over his ears all the way to Sutter's house if Cluke didn't shut up.

SUTTER'S HOUSE HAD one window and sat behind a line of trees. He probably heard Cluke singing as we walked up to the porch because the door opened, and he walked out without his shirt and shoes. Jesse asked him how he had been getting along. Sutter said he was fine. I told him what Mr. Moffett said about Sara. He said he didn't work for Mr. Moffett any more, and Sara was much better thanks to the new doctor in Sparta County. Sutter told us the doctor gave him the medicine Sara needed for a basket of eggs. Then Sutter said he had to go because she was calling his name. He walked into the house and closed the door behind him.

Jesse said he didn't hear Sara's voice, but Cluke said he did. Jesse asked me if I heard Sara's voice. I told him I wasn't really listening. As we turned toward the road to head home, Jesse stopped and told me that he wasn't crazy, and he knew when he heard a human voice and when he didn't, and if Sara called Sutter, one of us would have heard it. I told him that Cluke heard it, but he said that Cluke didn't count. Jesse frowned and scratched his head. He told me he had a sensible head on his shoulders, and he wasn't going to let Mr. Moffett and Sutter confuse his mind with lies when he knew Sara died about a month ago from the cough. Jesse bet me two dollars that if we walked over to that graveyard, we'd find Sara buried there. I told Jesse I wasn't much in the mood for betting after such a long day of walking. He said I didn't want to bet him because I knew I would lose. I told Jesse that maybe Sutter heard a ghost. He told me he didn't believe in ghosts, but Cluke said he did.

WE FINALLY MADE it to Main Street without Cluke giving us any problems. Jesse pointed at Little Chaney standing in Sutter's face holding a baseball bat in his hand. Sutter wiped blood from the side of his face and wiped it on his dirty shirt. We tried to get closer, but Big Chaney warned the crowd not to move. He lifted up his shirt, and we saw his pistol tucked in his pants. Cluke didn't understand why we couldn't move. We stood there pulling him back while he tried to move forward.

Jesse asked Sutter what he was doing. Sutter told him he wanted to sign up for that caboose race. Little Chaney told him that it was too late. Big Chaney just laughed and told Sutter to go home. Sutter said no.

Little Chaney moved closer to Sutter. "My brother said go home, Sutter."

"I want to run. I've got to win that prize money," Sutter said.

"I'm going to count to three. One," said Little Chaney.

"Go on home," Jesse said.

"I'm not going nowhere. I want to run in the caboose race."

"You better listen boy…Two!"

"Don't be a fool, Sutter. You don't want to cause any trouble around here," Jesse told Sutter.

"Fly, Sutter! They can't catch you if you fly away," said Cluke.

Little Chaney never said three. He swung the bat and hit Sutter on his head. Sutter went down on his knees. A line of blood ran down the side of his face and puddled at the collar of his shirt.

"Stay down, Sutter! Stay down," said Jesse.

"Get up, Sutter!" Jesse looked at me like I was making the situation worse than what it was.

"I've got a right to run in that caboose race," Sutter said.

"You ain't got no rights. All we got are rules around here, and the rule says you can't run in the caboose race. It looks like everybody can remember that except you," said Little Chaney. Sutter tried to rise to his feet again. Big Chaney pushed him down with his foot.

"Get up, Sutter," I said.

"You'd better thank God I didn't shoot you dead," said Big Chaney.

"I have a right to run in that caboose race," Sutter said. Big Chaney looked at Sutter and shook his head.

"Folks, everything is settled. This boy is crazy, that's all. Go on home and rest up for the caboose race tomorrow." Little Chaney followed Big Chaney into the hardware store and one of them put up the sign that said "closed."

"Sutter, are you all right?" I asked. "Help him get to his feet, Jesse."

Jesse didn't move.

"Help him get to his feet, Jesse."

"No. Leave me alone," Sutter said.

"We can't leave you here. We've got to get you to a doctor," Jesse told him.

"It won't do no good to go see a doctor in Moon County if you don't have the money to pay him. He'll just leave you there, waiting."

"Ain't too many men around here who'd stand up to Little Chaney the way you did," I said.

"But nothing changed. Nothing is ever going to change around here, and Sara is going to die!" Sutter was on his knees.

"Sara is already dead," said Jesse. "You're talking like you need to be in the asylum." Sutter scratched his head. He looked at the people standing on the sidewalk staring at him. He turned and watched me tightening the rope around Cluke's waist. He cried. "Don't do that. Leave him alone."

"But I have to tie him, or else Old Judge Delahunt will send him back to the asylum," I told him. Sutter looked up at the sky. He dropped his head.

"You hear that voice?" I frowned when he asked the question.

"What voice?" asked Jesse. "I don't hear anything."

"I don't hear anything either," I said.

"You hear it, don't you, Mr. Cluke. You hear what I'm hearing, don't you?" Cluke nodded.

"It's God talking. He said that the fox and the rabbit were friends, but the rabbit jumped out while the fox stayed in." Cluke laughed like it was the funniest thing he had ever heard in his life.

"Mr. Cluke, I think you might be right. It is God." Sutter wiped the blood from his lips and laughed.

"I hear God talk all the time," said Cluke.

"Cluke, we ain't got time for all of your foolishness," Jesse said. "Sutter, you ain't thinking right. You need to get to a doctor.

He'll tend to you. You just got to talk to him real respectful, that's all. Let him know he's the one with the upper hand."

"They'll be finished with that new hospital real soon, and you won't have to wait for a doctor like you do now. They'll have doctors for everybody," I told Sutter.

"I don't believe that will change things. I took Sara to see a doctor and no matter how much blood she coughed up, he always told her she just needed some rest. He never examined her, because I didn't have the money to pay him. Doctors will let you die if you don't have the money to pay them."

Sutter held his handkerchief against his head as he walked down Main Street. We pulled Cluke along and listened to him mumble his song. Jesse said the song still didn't make any sense to him. Sutter turned around once and looked at us like he couldn't focus his eyes. He dug into his pockets and pulled out some change. "Right here in my hand is all the money I've got. It's all I have left to give to Sara, but she's not here no more. What can I buy, now that she's not here no more?" Sutter asked us.

"You might be able to get a piece of sweet potato pie. You get the napkins for free. Don't you, Earl?" asked Cluke.

"Well, Mr. Cluke, that sounds like a reasonable thing to do with this money. I'm going to see if I can buy myself a piece of sweet potato pie," said Sutter.

Sutter turned around and walked up to the restaurant on the corner.

"You can't go through the front door. We're not allowed. We'll have to go to the back," Jesse said.

Sutter ignored him and marched right through the front door. We walked to the back of the restaurant. The owner brought Sutter out by the collar of his shirt and told him where he was supposed to go. Sutter didn't say a word.

We ordered sandwiches at the window. Cluke took out all of the change in his pockets and told me to buy him a piece of sweet potato pie. We sat on the ground watching Sutter eat his pie and stare at the dirt. Cluke finished eating his pie and started filling his pockets with rocks. Sutter looked at him, and he started filling his pockets with rocks, too. Jesse asked Sutter where he was going, but Sutter never said one word. We followed him farther down Main Street, stopping along the way so he and Cluke could pick up rocks and put them in their pockets.

By the time we reached the Oconee River, Cluke had a pocket full of rocks and so did Sutter. I whispered to Jesse that I thought Sutter was going to jump into the river. He said Sutter had better sense than that. Sutter kept walking and Cluke kept talking about how he was hungry and wanted to have fox and sweet potato pie for dinner. I promised him he could eat all the sweet potato pie he wanted to keep him from having a conniption, but I told him that most people didn't eat foxes. Cluke asked me why. He said that people ate rabbits. Jesse frowned at us both and told me I made it worse by trying to explain things to Cluke when I knew it would get all twisted in his head. Jesse said explaining life to Cluke was a waste of time. We moved closer to the river and watched Sutter walk along the bank. I asked him what he was going to do. He didn't answer. Cluke started to sing one of his songs; then Jesse put his hand over his mouth and Cluke bit it. Sutter just stared at us.

Just when we were all quiet enough to hear the crickets, Sutter jumped into the river. We stood there watching him fight the currents. Cluke tried to jump into the river, too, but me and Jesse pulled him back. He screamed and it echoed. Then Cluke got quiet. I pointed to his wet pants. Jesse threw his arms in the air and let out a deep breath. I told him that at least we knew Sutter could swim the currents. Jesse said that it didn't matter because there was no way Sutter was ever going to run in the long-car caboose race.

Nobody in Moon County was sure who would win that last race. Most folks had placed their bets on Motor Ross, the human engine. He was the best runner and swimmer around. He was the only man to ever win the race three times in a row. He could run with his shoes, or without them. He could swim for miles without getting tired. Everybody knew that Motor Ross could easily beat Charlie Watson, Stanley Turner, Shed Morgan, and Bobby Joe Tateman. I placed bets on all four of them, just to be safe.

Me, Cluke, and Jesse gathered on the hill with the crowd. The train curved into the cow pasture at two o'clock. Big Chaney fired the pistol, and Motor Ross shot past all the others in a flash. Shed wasn't too far behind him. Stanley was running a strong third. Then, out of nowhere, came Sutter, running past Charlie and Bobby Joe in the rear. Seeing Sutter running in the long-car caboose race was like a dream. I was proud, but Jesse wasn't. He was afraid some folks in the crowd wouldn't like it, because Sutter was breaking the rules, but nobody said or did anything. We all just stood there watching as Sutter ran past Stanley and Shed, but he couldn't seem to get past Motor Ross. Motor Ross made it to the caboose, and Motor Ross kicked at Sutter as he reached for something to hold on to. Finally, Sutter grabbed the side of the caboose and didn't let go. They fought all the way to the bridge; then the two of them dropped into the Oconee River. Motor Ross made it back to the finish line. Sutter didn't.

ODESSA

There was not one thing wrong with the Crawford family name in Moon County until my older sister, Fancy, became a cashier at the five-n-dime and started letting Lady Estella read her palms and put crazy ideas in her head. Lady Estella told Fancy that a man would cause a fortunate event to take place in her life. Nobody but Fancy would get all excited about some love lie that would probably never come true.

Everybody in the house knew when Fancy had been at Lady Estella's. Supper would be late, and Uncle Paul would get the headache because he couldn't take his pills on an empty stomach. Our daddy, Deacon Charlie, would be missing clean shirts from his closet or the day's paper would still be on the porch. Without the day's paper, I would never be able to keep up with the comings and goings in Moon County. Like last month, when the Midnight Bandit showed up here, and the paper ran the story on the front page with a sketch of his face and all kinds of personal description. It threw everybody into a fit of fear. Folks were scared to sit on their porches, but that didn't stop Deacon Charlie from sitting in his porch rocker and enjoying his Bible. He just loaded up one of those old pistols he kept in the attic and held it in his lap. Deacon Charlie loved the church, and he loaned one gun apiece to all the other deacons.

Things had to be pretty terrible in Moon County if Deacon Charlie felt he had to loan out a gun. Of course, most things that scared a normal Crawford just terrified Fancy. She slept on the floor in Deacon Charlie's room for a week because he slept with a pistol under his pillow. But do you think having a criminal on the loose kept Fancy from walking alone to the five-n-dime every morning and staying until dark at Lady Estella's house wasting perfectly good five-dollar bills? Sure didn't. Being a Crawford, you would think Fancy had the good taste to pretend to know better, but she never listened to a word Deacon Charlie told her. She said Lady Estella told her she didn't have to listen to men.

Deacon Charlie always said Fancy was the selfish one in the family. I thoroughly agreed, and this was exactly why I told Fancy she would probably end up worse than our Cousin Addie. It really takes Deacon Charlie to tell you the whole story about Cousin Addie. She was so crazy they had to send her to live on Cherokee Island. It's the land in the middle of the Oconee River where folks go for vacation. It used to be where they sent the outcasts until the asylum was built. Cousin Addie eventually got moved there, and she lived to be an eighty-year-old bird feeder. Deacon Charlie said that's just what happened to crazy women back in the old days.

Do you think Fancy paid attention to what Deacon Charlie said about Cousin Addie? Sure didn't. I don't think I told you about the time Fancy came home from Lady Estella's at ten o'clock at night knowing good and well Uncle Paul had to take his pills before six. Uncle Paul takes all kinds of pills, and he has a crowd of doctors and a hat box full of unpaid bills. He has seen every doctor in Moon County and Sparta County about his headaches. You can catch him at his best health after church services and in the spring when he sells lemonade on the corner. If you want Uncle Paul to like you, just ask him about caboose racing or that blue ribbon he won for eating fifty eggs at the Moon County fair. Deacon Charlie always said Uncle Paul was the talker in the family. I thoroughly disagreed. Just mention the name Mr. Reese and you'd have to throw Fancy into afternoon traffic on Main Street just to shut her up.

Mr. Reese was Fancy's artificial lover. Fancy denied it. She said there was no such thing, and that it was just something else I was using to make Deacon Charlie go against her for seeing Lady Estella. There most certainly was such a thing as an artificial lover. I read all about it in the newspaper while I was waiting in Dr. Pike's office. We had to drive all the way to Sparta County to see Dr. Pike because Uncle Paul swore he was the only doctor in the state of Georgia who could treat him for diarrhea. Well, there was a newspaper in Dr. Pike's office, and on page ten was an article on how grieving humans invent folks to take the place of dead loved ones. It was real psychology. My teacher talked about psychology all the time. A person like Fancy would never understand something like that. I read that article twice to make sure I had the meaning straight.

When I told Fancy that Mr. Reese was her artificial lover, she put up a wall of defense worse than Uncle Paul did when Dr. Pike told him he needed to see a head doctor. I told her Mr. Reese was artificial just as sure as the day was long, and that God would strike her with a bolt of lightning on a sunny day if she kept telling love lies.

"Mr. Reese is not artificial, Odessa. I suspect I'll have to have Deacon Charlie get the switch after you if you say another word against me."

"Then how come nobody has ever seen him? Lady Estella has been telling you for weeks that Mr. Reese was coming. Deacon Charlie wants to meet him."

"There's no need to be all anxious. Deacon Charlie will meet him any day now. Lady Estella says you can't rush good fortune. Patience is a woman's greatest virtue," said Fancy as she banged pots and pans and slammed cabinet doors, trying to get supper ready before Deacon Charlie and Uncle Paul got home from the barbershop. She sat plates on the newspaper I had spread out on the table just when I was getting to the good part about how the Midnight Bandit was all laid up in the hospital because Deacon Morris shot him in the arm when he tried to break into his house.

"It says right here that Deacon Morris held the Midnight Bandit at gunpoint until the sheriffs came and arrested both of them. They got one for attempted robbery and the other for carrying somebody else's gun."

"You don't have to tell me everything. I read it. Come help me with supper."

"You can't tell me what to do."

"I most certainly can. Deacon Charlie told me that I'm the woman of the house now, and I have to teach you how to be one too."

"You know Deacon Morris has that heart condition that momma had. It's just shameful the way that sheriff locked him up."

"So what? Folks go to the jailhouse every day. Deacon Morris is no different. Lady Estella says it will do him plenty good to feel what it's like to be on the other side of justice. Lady Estella has one of those special minds. You're too young to understand a woman like her. She knows her rights."

"Well, it says here that the Midnight Bandit will go straight to the jailhouse next week when they release him from that new hospital they just finished building."

"So what. They should have built a hospital in Moon County years ago. If you don't come help me with supper, I'm going to tell Deacon Charlie to get the switch after you."

WHEN WE ALL finally sat down at the table to sort through the Wednesday leftovers Fancy threw together and called supper, she started explaining to Deacon Charlie why there were no clean shirts hanging in his closet. "Oh, I was late coming home from the five-n-dime. Mr. Tile likes for us to help him count the stock."

"This ham don't taste right. It tastes old," hollered Uncle Paul.

"The ham is perfectly fine, you sour fool. I think it is best you shut up and eat if you want to take your pills."

"It is too late, and who says you can talk to me like that? Deacon Charlie, you hear how Fancy just talked?" asked Uncle Paul.

"It's that Lady Estella woman," I said.

"Deacon Charlie, don't listen to them," she said.

"Well, you know that's not her real name," said Deacon Charlie. "Her real name is Beatrice—Beatrice Robinson. Only God knows why she started calling herself Lady Estella."

"She ain't no lady either. I've seen goats with more manners than that woman," said Uncle Paul.

"She is too," said Fancy.

"This ham don't taste right. I know something is wrong with this ham," said Uncle Paul.

"It's left over, Uncle Paul. Fancy is too lazy to cook a fresh meal."

"I suspect I need to beg your pardon, Odessa, seeing how you want to be all grown up, but you don't lift a finger to help around this house. Deacon Charlie, don't you think it's about time Odessa took on her share of responsibilities around here now that I am a career woman?"

"You know your cousin David ran a farm and raised ten children all by himself after Eugenia died. God knows Eugenia sure was a sweet woman. Sweet as can be, that Eugenia. Odessa, help your sister."

"But I wasn't the one who told Fancy she had to go out and get a job in the first place; was I, Uncle Paul?"

"It was you, Deacon Charlie. There's no denying it. I heard you tell her with my own ears," said Uncle Paul. "It's that Lady Estella that's got her talking this way. Months ago, you wouldn't even know Fancy was in the house. Now, every day, she comes in late and brings in a thunderstorm with her. I haven't taken my pills on time in two weeks."

"That's not my fault," said Fancy.

"See. You hear that, Deacon Charlie? You hear that talk? It's disrespectful. That's what it is. And this is the worst supper I ever had in my life. It's worse than the worst. I'm never going to eat Fancy's cooking again."

"If that's the way you want it, fine then. You could drop dead right this minute of starvation of the stomach and see if I care. I suspect it's time for me to make my departure from this table and eat my supper in my room. I wish not to be bothered for the rest of my life, thank you very much."

As soon as Fancy was out of the room, Uncle Paul was stretched spread eagle on the kitchen floor hollering about food poisoning and having his stomach pumped. It scared every last one of us worse than the Midnight Bandit. So we all rushed Uncle Paul to the new hospital and it's clean and lovely. Fancy said she was sorry and tried to take back those words she said to Uncle Paul. The only person who forgave her was Deacon Charlie.

We sat in the waiting room for hours flipping through magazines and admiring everything. But do you think Fancy calmed down and prayed for forgiveness from God like Deacon Charlie told her to? Sure didn't. Fancy asked the nurse whether Uncle Paul was going to die of food poisoning about a hundred times. To keep Fancy from asking so many questions, the nurse told her that maybe she should walk around the hospital to calm her nerves.

Do you remember that fortunate event that Lady Estella said would happen to Fancy? Well, Fancy said it happened right there in the hospital. Of course, none of us saw it. While we were waiting in the visiting room drinking coffee and reading, Fancy was walking all around the hospital playing Ms. Nosey and came face-to-face with the Midnight Bandit in the women's bathroom. Fancy made me swear on the Bible and promised me her week's pay if I would not tell Deacon Charlie about the incident. She said she recognized the Midnight Bandit the minute he stepped out of the stall dressed up like some janitor.

I asked her if she was scared out of her natural-born mind. What she said sounded like something straight out of Lady Estella's mouth. Fancy said she saw his face and looked into those eyes of his and saw instant love. Fancy told me he looked exactly like Mr. Reese when he winked his left eye at her. I didn't believe a word of her story until I caught her sneaking out the back door with a suitcase later that night.

"Fancy, just where do you think you're going at this time of the night?"

"I'm running away with the Midnight Bandit. He asked me to go with him to Chattanooga."

"What! Fancy, are you out of your natural-born mind? You've never lived outside Moon County a day in your life."

"That doesn't matter. Guess what he told me at that hospital, Odessa?"

"What?"

"He said I was the most beautiful woman he'd ever seen in the whole wide world, and he wants to spend the rest of his life with me."

"For God's sake, Fancy, what do you expect a man on the loose to say. Where is he? I'll get Deacon Charlie to go shoot him."

"He is waiting for me over at Lady Estella's. I told him to go there to be safe."

"What am I supposed to tell Deacon Charlie?"

"Nothing. You promised me you wouldn't tell. Lady Estella says silence is a woman's greatest virtue."

IF YOU ASK ME, Fancy didn't stay away long enough for anybody to really miss her. Sure, Deacon Charlie asked me a thousand questions about why Fancy left home. I told him I didn't know, but I don't think he believed a word I said. Uncle Paul said it would do Fancy plenty of good to get away from Lady Estella. I agreed. Uncle Paul was not around the house much, because Dr. Pike drove over from Sparta County one day and arranged to have him committed to a two-week program at the asylum. He got his own room and his own personal attendant. Uncle Paul went into a rage when he realized he couldn't come home. It took three attendants to strap him to his bed. After a day or two, he started to like it a little. He said the cooking at the asylum was better than Fancy's.

For the first time, there was peace and quiet in the Crawford house. The ladies at the church took turns coming over to cook and clean because I wasn't lifting a finger. The place was a mess the week Deacon Morris was found dead in his living room just two days after he was released from the jailhouse and fined for carrying Deacon Charlie's gun. The doctor said Deacon Morris died of a massive heart attack. His obituary was printed on the front page of the newspaper along with the story about the Midnight Bandit being captured and locked up in the Sparta State Prison.

Of course, Fancy showed up at the funeral in the same dress she left in the night she ran away with the Midnight Bandit. She pitched the biggest fit over Deacon Morris. It was much more embarrassing than anything Uncle Paul ever did. Everybody forgot about the wife, and looked at Fancy on her knees screaming about dedicating the rest of her life to serving the will of God. Folks didn't know whether to cry or clap for her. Then Deacon Charlie went over to help her up, and he gave her a big hug. Fancy slept for two days, and Deacon Charlie made me promise to be nice to her. That was harder than I thought because she was always trying to tell me what to do. Fancy took a leave of absence from her job at the five-n-dime, and said she wanted to spend her time serving Jesus. She promised Deacon Charlie she wouldn't go back to Lady Estella's. Instead, she rushed off to every Bible study or church meeting there was. Fancy even joined the choir, knowing perfectly well no Crawford could ever carry a tune. Deacon Charlie loved every bit of it and suggested that I become a woman of the church, too.

Uncle Paul eventually came home, but he still had to go to group counseling every Wednesday. Sometimes, we all went. This was Fancy's idea. I thoroughly disagreed, but she told Deacon Charlie that we should support each other more. It was a lot like being in church on Sunday. The only thing was that folks had to talk about themselves instead of God. We all got along real fine until Fancy caught that virus that she said was going around. Fancy couldn't start the morning without spending twenty minutes in the bathroom.

"Deacon Charlie, I do believe I must have caught the virus. I hear it is going around," said Fancy at the kitchen table.

"I ain't heard about a virus," said Uncle Paul.

"Whatever you got, I hope it's not contagious," I said.

"Don't worry Odessa. You'd have to go to bed with a man to get what Fancy has," said Uncle Paul.

"What are you saying there, Uncle Paul?" asked Deacon Charlie.

"I suspect I need to beg your pardon, Uncle Paul, seeing how you don't know a thing about a woman's body."

"You can't fool me. I know the signs of science," said Uncle Paul.

"What signs?" asked Deacon Charlie.

"Deacon Charlie, I think Uncle Paul is saying Fancy is going to have a baby," I said.

"Shut up, Odessa," said Fancy.

"With no husband in sight, I might add," said Uncle Paul.

"Shut up, Uncle Paul. You sour fool."

"Listen at how she talked. Deacon Charlie, I thought you said Fancy changed. She hasn't changed one bit and now she's got this bastard child coming to the world by God knows who. Just shameful that's all. I'm glad my sister is not around here to witness the bad example you're setting for Odessa."

"Well, Fancy, what do you have to say for yourself?" asked Deacon Charlie.

"That's just some more of Uncle Paul's nonsense talk. Even if I was with child, I have no earthly idea how it happened."

"Don't play innocent. You know how it happened. Ain't but one way. You can't fool me," said Uncle Paul. "I know what you were doing while you were gone."

"I beg you not to put words in my mouth. There are plenty of other ways to get pregnant."

"Name one," I said.

"Immaculate conception!"

"My teacher says there is no such thing!" I said.

"How do you think we got Jesus?" Fancy asked me.

"There is no need for you to be dragging the good name of the Lord into the mess you made. That's blaspheming if I ever heard it," said Uncle Paul.

"Just ask Deacon Charlie, if you don't believe me."

"That sounds like something Lady Estella told you to say. You promised Deacon Charlie you wouldn't go to Lady Estella's anymore," I said.

"Lady Estella didn't tell me anything. I got it from the Bible, thank you very much. Tell them, Deacon Charlie."

"Fancy is right. It happened in the Bible, to Mary, the mother of the Lord."

"Fancy ain't no Mary!" said Uncle Paul. "She might be Mary Magdalene, but she ain't Mary, the mother of the Lord."

"Are you calling me a liar in my own house?" asked Deacon Charlie.

"No, but if you let Fancy get away with dragging the Bible through the mud, I'm moving to Sparta County with Dr. Pike, and I'm going to live under false identification."

"Nobody's going anywhere until we all go to the hospital to get everything checked out," said Deacon Charlie.

When we got to the hospital, the doctor paid more attention to Uncle Paul than Fancy. The minute we walked through the door, Uncle Paul started complaining about chest pains and an ingrown toenail. The doctor admitted him right on the spot.

After Uncle Paul was released, he told everybody in Moon County that the doctor said Fancy was going to have a bastard child. Well, the doctor didn't say the word "bastard." Uncle Paul added that part later. Of course, Deacon Charlie and Fancy told everybody the baby was a miracle from God.

And if you must know the details of how all this turned out, Fancy told Deacon Charlie that she thought it was a good idea if I held her job at the five-n-dime while school was out for the summer. I thoroughly disagreed, but Deacon Charlie didn't. Because I was going to be an aunt, he thought I should take on more responsibility, which sounded like something Fancy probably told him to tell me.

Working at the five-n-dime was just like going to church. You always got a chance to see everybody you didn't want to see. Folks made all kinds of jokes about the family. Some of them asked me when I was going to give Deacon Charlie another grandchild. The part about the marriage before the baby carriage didn't even matter anymore, thanks to Fancy. She sure set some fine example for me to follow.

Folks thought I knew anything and everything about her just because we were sisters. I couldn't make it through the day without folks asking questions about Fancy's baby being the child of a convict. Honestly, who could be mean enough to start a nasty rumor like that? Folks asked me all the time what I thought about it. I told them to go ask Lady Estella because only she could tell for sure whether Moon County should be expecting a future criminal, or a saint, or somebody between the two.

SONNY AND CLEOPHUS

My name is Sonny, and I'm a prisoner. When I came to the Sparta State Prison, I was told one of the questions the Parole Committee would ask you during your parole hearing was whether or not you were ready to enter back into society. When it was time for me to have my hearing to answer that question, I told the committee yes. Lucky for you, I didn't get paroled. If I did, there would be no point in telling you this story.

I don't like to talk about my conviction, but you ought to know a little about how I ended up in the pen at the ripe old age of eighteen. I was always in and out of trouble growing up. What got me a ten-year sentence was a grocery store robbery gone bad. My girl Daisy waited in the motorcar while I went into the store early one Friday morning. I pointed the gun at the nervous old rooster standing behind the register. I told him to hand over the money or I'd shoot him. I wished you could have seen how bad he was sweating. He kept talking about how I was making a mistake, and that I could make a better life for myself if I just worked hard. I told him to shut the hell up because I didn't believe that anymore, and I felt really sorry for anybody who did.

2.

THAT OLD ROOSTER never knew I didn't have the guts to shoot him. Something in me just wouldn't let me kill another human being. He probably called the Moon County sheriff soon as I ran out with the money. Daisy drove the motorcar as fast as she could, but she lost control of it. It ended up crashing into a tree, and Daisy went through the windshield. She died instantly. I busted up my head on the side. After a short stay in the hospital, with a sheriff put on duty to watch my every move, I was taken to the courthouse and charged with burglary and assault; then I was dressed in prison clothes along with the six other "new fish" and escorted to a bus headed to Sparta State Prison. I sat in the seat with the man who ended up being my cellmate. Everybody called him Squeak because that was what his voice sounded like when he talked. He had a thin moustache and a bad case of the shakes. I wished you could have seen him. He told me he was charged with rape, but it was hard for me to believe a man that nervous could rape anybody. He mentioned something about his classification papers; then he asked me what I was in for. I told him that it wasn't rape and he looked at me like he was trying to figure out my crime. He asked me if I was scared to be locked up, and I said no. I told him I wasn't scared of anything, especially not a dump like the Sparta State Prison.

The prison was located out in an open field. It was basically a pile of bricks stacked two stories high and wrapped in yards of fence. Inside, there were lights that made the long halls look clean and bright, but the place smelled like piss and musty bodies. Inmates moved about mingling, staring, and hissing. When the guards took me and Squeak down to our cellblock, I felt like a dog going into a cage. The cell had a tiny window on the back wall. With the stained toilet and sink on one side of the cell, and the stacked bunks on the other side, there wasn't much room for two bodies. Squeak walked in. He sat on the bottom bunk and covered his face with his hands. I couldn't do anything but stand there watching him shake like he was freezing.

The guard wearing the name tag that said "Briggs" locked us in. He said, "Welcome home, ladies. Standing count is at six in the morning, four in the afternoon, and nine at night."

3.

THERE WERE TWO kinds of laws in the Sparta State Prison. There was the official law the state government put in place for the people who ran the joint; then there was the unofficial law made by the inmates themselves. It didn't take me long to realize I was surrounded by some of the finest criminal minds in the state of Georgia. After the guards put me and Squeak in our cell, it seemed like all the men in our cellblock came to look us over. Of course, they called us all kinds of country heck and pretty boy sissy names and asked us what we were in for. Like a fool, Squeak told them he was in for raping some girl. I kept quiet because I knew better. Both of our crimes together couldn't stack up against the convictions those inmates called out.

The old rooster with the thick eyeglasses and beard was Booker. He was locked up years ago for killing two men in a bank robbery. He kept staring at me and scribbling on a notepad. The one making the most noise was Moses. If you saw Moses, you'd never want to see him again. He was all mean frowns and muscles, and his arms reminded me of a sledge hammer. Moses said that he beat two men to death by himself because they tried to cheat him in a racket. He grabbed the bars to the cell and told me and Squeak that we belonged to him.

Then just when I thought I'd be dead before I even made it to my first parole hearing, an old man with a bald head and a patch over his right eye pushed through the crowd with a book cart. He stared at me like he knew me. He told Moses that he could have Squeak, but I belonged to him. The man reached through the bars and handed me a book with an Indian on the cover. He said that his name was Cleophus.

4.

ONE OF THE HONORS you got for good behavior in the Sparta State Prison was a cushy work detail in the library. Mr. Boyer was the librarian and the warden's brother-in-law. His teeth were mossy and he combed his hair over his bald spot. Cleophus said he taught Boyer everything he knew about the library because everybody knew Boyer only got the job because of his family connections. Cleophus said as long as he took care of the library, Boyer took care of him.

The prison library had more books in it than my high school. I walked up and down the aisles looking. A small stepladder was kept at the end of each stack because the shelves were made high so that there would be more room for books. I spent the first week learning how to catalog books and how to read the letters and numbers on the binding to put them in order. Cleophus said stacking the books on the shelves always went much faster when two people worked together.

He gave me the rundown on who ran things around the place. First of all, the guards couldn't be trusted, even though there were a few like Briggs who cut deals on the side for extra cash. If they ever came around asking a lot of questions about another inmate, you went limp on them. One of the worst things you could ever let one of them hear you say was that you were innocent. They beat the hell out of inmates for that all the time. Cleophus told me to stay away from Chaplain Gregory, because he was always talking about God and conversion. One time Cleophus told Chaplain Gregory there were four Gods up in heaven, and Chaplain Gregory had to be rushed to the infirmary to have his heart monitored. When he got out, Cleophus said Chaplain Gregory told him that he needed to see the psychiatrist, but Cleophus said all the psychiatrist ever wanted to talk about was rehabilitation.

No money equals no power in prison, but if you had money, Cleophus said that you could go down the cellblock line and buy pretty much anything you wanted. Short Tate could get you hard liquor, uppers, downers, or reefer cigarettes. Mann Ann could get you a private meeting with one of the ladies over in the cellblock that everybody called Babylon. Dirty Johnny could get you dirty magazines and women's panties. Booker could give you a loan and run numbers for you. Booker and Cleophus were the last of the old-timers still around. Cleophus got him to get me the work transfer to the library and out of the laundry room where Squeak ended up.

I don't think Squeak had any idea how hard things were going to be for him in that laundry. He was laid up in the infirmary by the end of his second day of work. Moses and a few of his buddies put him there because they thought he needed to know what rape felt like. They might have torn up his butt a little, but his mind was the thing that got shot to pieces. Squeak never talked after that. It was hard for me to even look at the poor bastard without feeling sorry for him and thanking God I wasn't in his shoes. Every time cell bars slammed or somebody yelled, Squeak jumped like a firecracker went off beside him. Cleophus said that was a sign of a man who'd never make it to his first parole hearing. "Sometimes, it only takes a few minutes to ruin a man's life forever," he said.

Cleophus loved coming up with proverbs, especially when he wasn't hounding me about reading the book on Indians he gave me, or nosing around in my life. He asked me a lot of questions, and he wouldn't stop until he got an answer that satisfied him. The first thing he hounded me about was how I ended up in prison so young. I asked him why he wanted to know. All I got was a proverb: "If you can't figure out how you ended up in here, you'll keep coming back. Life is like that."

5.

BECAUSE THERE WASN'T much else to do in prison, I spent most of my time daydreaming and thinking about what I could tell Cleophus to get him to stop asking me so many questions. Cleophus said he asked a lot of questions to keep life from getting too boring. He said, "Learn how to occupy your time and time won't occupy you." That was Cleophus for you, always dishing proverbs when all I wanted him to do was give me a cigarette to smoke after lunch.

6.

"HOW DO YOU THINK Squeak is holding up?" I asked Cleophus while we sat at the table in the dining hall.

"I think his soul is broken, and prison is not the place to have a broken soul. You've got folks around here like Booker who like to believe they're insurance salesmen. The other day, I was asking him about the money he owed me. He said he thinks Squeak will be dead by the third week of this month. That's what a lot of folks are betting on. Is he still not talking?"

"He hasn't said one word since he got out of the infirmary. He cries at night like a big baby."

"What do you do at night? I know you're not reading that book I gave you."

"I sleep with the pillow over my head. I'm nobody's babysitter," I told him.

"You don't cry?"

"Hell no! What do I have to cry about?"

"Oh, I imagine you might have a lot of things to cry about. If my daddy left me, my momma, and my brother with no money, there would be plenty for me to cry about."

"Were you listening to what I told you or not? I told you it was my daddy's brother, Uncle Will, who cut out on his family."

"Yeah, right, and I've got a glass eye coming Pony Express tomorrow," said Cleophus.

7.

WE WALKED BACK to the library from the dining hall with Briggs walking behind us watching every move we made. Cleophus got a big kick out of the fact that I was starting to open up a little. Once I told him everything, he promised to stop asking so many questions. He wanted me to start back at the beginning because he claimed he heard it all wrong the first time.

I told him that my Uncle Will decided he wasn't in love with my Aunt Mary anymore, so he cut out on her and the children.

They had two boys. The family didn't know what to do, because they were about to lose everything. My daddy liked to run the show, so he called this big gathering in our kitchen so the family could have a meeting of the minds. The only problem was the minds in our family didn't like to meet. Daddy sat at the head of the table rubbing the stubbles on his face. Momma sat beside him. I wondered how she was going to divide a bowl of peas between us and our kinfolks sitting around the kitchen table. She had long hair, but she wore it pinned up to keep it out of her face while she worked around the house. I wished you could have seen the two of them sitting there. What Daddy said with his mouth, Momma could say with the expression on her face.

"Well, we've got to figure out who is going to take in Will's boys. Any volunteers?" asked Daddy. Aunt Ellen didn't say a word, knowing she had plenty of room in her house because she and Uncle Roger had a little money, and they never had any children. I wished you could have seen Aunt Ellen sitting at the table. She wore a hat. She loved hats, and she wore one everywhere she went, even at the table. She sat at the table and held her pocketbook close to her chest because my brother Cabbage had a real bad habit of sneaking it away from her and stealing her dimes and peppermint. Aunt Ellen always said that Cabbage was a child marked for no good because he had a birthmark on his forehead.

8.

"WHAT WAS the birthmark shaped like?" asked Cleophus after he reached into a box and handed me a stack of donated books to stack on the shelf. "You know how, sometimes, you can have a birthmark and it is shaped like something? My brother Joe Henry had one on his back shaped like a boot."

"It really didn't have a shape to me. My momma always said it looked like a cabbage leaf. Aunt Ellen always said it reminded her of Cain in the Bible."

"How old was Cabbage when he started stealing?" asked Cleophus.

"I can't remember exactly."

"Where did he learn to be a thief?"

"If you ever let me finish the story, you might find out." One of the books fell. When I leaned over to pick it up, I noticed Cleophus staring at me with a blank look on his face.

"Go right ahead. I'm listening."

9.

MY DADDY SAID Cabbage got his thieving ways from Momma's side of the family. Momma said he got them from me, and that I should be setting a better example for him because I was the oldest. Aunt Ellen told Momma that she didn't believe I could set a good example for Cabbage; then she repeated how she felt about Aunt Mary and her boys. Momma stared at Aunt Ellen. Aunt Ellen held on to that pocketbook with her fist balled. Cabbage stood at Aunt Ellen's side waiting for somebody to ask her about her cancer. When somebody asked her that question, she dropped her pocketbook and got herself ready to brawl.

Uncle Tuck just sat there rubbing his thick beard. He kept looking around the table. I guess he didn't understand why he was there.

10.

"WHAT ABOUT YOU, Tuck?" asked Daddy.

"Me and Bea can barely keep food on the table for Colleen." He folded his arms and frowned.

"Well, Ellen, it looks like it's going to have to be you," said Daddy.

"No. I'm too sick to have children in my house. There's too much medication around. Plus, Roger doesn't like children," she said.

"He likes me," said Cabbage. He tried to touch Aunt Ellen's hat and she swatted at him with her hand.

"Hush up, Cabbage," Daddy said.

"Ellen, you've got more room in your house than the rest of us," Daddy told her.

Momma looked at Aunt Ellen the way she did when she was about to take a switch to Cabbage. I could tell a fire was starting in her because she kept rubbing her hands.

"Yeah, but none of you got cancer."

"What does that have to do with anything?" Momma asked, slamming her bowl of peas on the table.

"It has everything to do with it. I don't want to give those children the cancer," she said.

"My teacher said that cancer ain't contagious," I said. I did some quick figuring in my mind about how things were probably going to get played out if Momma got a chance to put her two cents in again.

"Sonny is right. Cancer ain't contagious. You just don't want to help, that's all," said Uncle Tuck.

"You shut up, you old rooster! I have a right to say no if I want to."

"Ellen, why are you being so selfish?" asked Daddy.

"I'm not being selfish."

"You are too," said Momma. "You're being a selfish old hen."

"Who are you calling a hen?" Aunt Ellen jumped to her feet and her pocketbook fell to the floor. Cabbage grabbed it. Before he could get his hand in it good, Aunt Ellen snatched it away from him. "Did you see what that little thief of yours just did?"

"Did you just call my child a thief?" asked Momma.

"I sure did. Sonny and Cabbage are both thieves, and everybody in Moon County knows they are just a breath away from being thrown in the reformatory!"

"I've had about enough of this foolishness. Get out of my house, Ellen," screamed Momma. Daddy rushed Aunt Ellen to the door with her pocketbook before a brawl started.

11.

"BUT ELLEN, what about Will's children?" asked Uncle Tuck.

"Send them to the reformatory for all I care. That's probably where they'll end up anyway," said Aunt Ellen. She marched down the steps of the porch. Daddy stood in the screened door with his jaw dropped.

"It's just not right to turn your back on your own family. Families are supposed to stick together," said Momma.

"Nobody's sending anybody to the reformatory. We'll take Mary and her boys in. I'll just have to find extra work. Money will be tight around here, but we'll make due with God's blessings," said Daddy.

"We can't afford it. We're already poor. Why can't you make them go live with Aunt Ellen?" I asked.

"We are not poor, Sonny. There are plenty of people with way less than we have," said Momma.

"Name one," I said. Daddy just looked at me and then at Cabbage.

"Yesterday in the store, Daddy told old Potter he didn't have any money to pay down our credit," said Cabbage. He grabbed some raw peas and dropped them into his mouth.

"Cabbage, didn't I tell you to keep your mouth closed about what took place between me and old Potter?" asked Daddy.

"See, even Cabbage knows I'm telling the truth," I told Momma. "We are poor, and we are going to be poor forever if you let them move in with us."

"What have I told you about being selfish? Go to your room and don't come out until you've asked God to forgive you for being so selfish," said Momma.

"But Momma, he didn't do anything," said Cabbage.

"You go with him, Cabbage. I've had about enough of you for one day," said Daddy.

"Why do I have to go?" Cabbage broke out in tears because he was just a big old baby anyway.

"You don't know how to keep your mouth shut, that's why," said Daddy.

12.

WHEN WE WERE SENT to our room, I knew things were settled. I could see what was coming next. Uncle Will's whole family was coming to live with us, and there would be more people and less of everything else. What we had was already close to nothing. I told Cabbage we had to map out a plan of action. I wished you could have seen him standing there dropping raw peas into his mouth.

"Ain't nothing we can do, Sonny," he said.

"Yes, there is. We can run away. They won't ever notice we're gone."

"Where will we go?"

"Sparta County."

"Daddy said that's where they send prisoners. Why do we have to go there?"

"It won't be long before things get really hard around here. One of us is going to end up in the reformatory. Do you want to go to the reformatory?"

"No, but how are we going to eat? We don't have any money."

"We'll put some food on daddy's credit at old Potter's grocery."

"But yesterday, old Potter told daddy that he couldn't put anything else on his credit until he paid it down," said Cabbage.

"Then we'll steal it," I said.

"Old Potter said if he ever caught us stealing again, he'd have the sheriff lock us up in the reformatory until we turned eighteen."

"No, he won't, Cabbage. Old Potter has been saying that for years. Daddy will go talk to him, and he'll drop the charges like he always does. Now cross your heart and promise that you'll keep this a secret."

"I promise."

"Swear to God."

"I swear to God and I hope to die, stick a needle in my eye," said Cabbage.

13.

CLEOPHUS AND I brought in more boxes of books from Boyer's office and pushed them against the wall so they could be unpacked and given catalog numbers. While I talked, Cleophus kept looking at me and frowning like he had tasted something sour.

"What is it? I can tell you're just dying to ask something. What is it?"

"You weren't just a little scaredy cat to run away from home? Not even a little?" asked Cleophus.

"Nope. I wasn't scared of anything then; and I ain't scared of anything now."

"You sound really brave," said Cleophus. "I don't think you were really that brave at all."

"I was brave. I come from a family of brave people."

"Whatever happened to Aunt Ellen?"

"She died."

"Well, whatever happened to Aunt Mary and her children?"

"They moved in, but a few months later Aunt Mary and her boys moved to Atlanta to live with her folks."

"What happened to Cabbage?" Cleophus asked.

"Just hold that question for a minute. I want to finish telling you how we ran away."

14.

I MAPPED THINGS OUT real good, so that me and Cabbage could get to Sparta County. Momma was already organizing things so Aunt Mary would have a room to herself, and her boys would get to sleep in the room with me and Cabbage. I couldn't even think about that without my stomach hurting. I knew daddy was probably going to have to do something besides drive that ice truck to make ends meet. So I kept planning. The shortest way to Sparta County was through the woods and east of the Oconee River. I told Cabbage we'd get ourselves a clean start in Sparta County and do whatever we wanted to do. Instead of going to school, we headed to old Potter's grocery store up on Main Street before the morning crowd started coming in.

15.

"WHO IS old Potter again?" asked Cleophus.

"He's the man who owned the store my daddy had credit with," I told him.

"What did he look like?"

"He had a bald head just like you, and instead of wearing a patch, he wore a dirty apron. His store always smelled like rotten onions. Momma hated buying things from him. She said old Potter kept his store too dirty."

"You can't always trust the way something looks. I learned that lesson after I lost my eye and had to start wearing this patch. I might have one eye, but I feel like I can see with four of them," said Cleophus. He stared at the book in his hand.

"This is a book I think you should read."

"What's it about?"

"It's about a man who wanders in the desert for a year and all the different people he meets. Somebody kills him in the end." I shook my head to let Cleophus know I wasn't interested in reading about some man dying in the desert. He handed the book to me and I put it on the shelf. Everything was quiet in the stacks until Cleophus asked me to finish telling him what happened when me and Cabbage got to old Potter's store. So I told him.

16.

OLD POTTER SCRATCHED his bald head and stared at me and Cabbage when we walked in. "Sonny, what are you and Cabbage doing in here this early on a school morning?"

"Our momma sent us to get some sugar before we went to school," Cabbage said.

"Well, you're on the wrong aisle. Sugar is over on three. You'd better hurry up. The school bell will be ringing in twenty minutes." Old Potter pointed to aisle three. I motioned for Cabbage to follow his aim while I cleaned up on candy bars.

Mr. Granger stumbled up the aisle smelling like gin. Flies swarmed around him. He pulled a flask out of his shirt pocket and took a long sip from it. He looked like he hadn't touched soap and water in days. I wished you could have seen him and those flies. He looked like something people paid a dollar to see at the Moon County fair.

"You got any velvet, old Potter? It's my wife's birthday. I want to buy her some velvet so she can make herself a fine dress like Mrs. Wick used to wear," he said.

"No, Mr. Granger, I will tell you again like I have been telling you for the last two days I don't sell velvet. I'm a grocer."

"I've got money. I've been saving. I know you have velvet to sell."

"Don't you cross my words, Mr. Granger. What have I told you about coming into my store drinking and bringing in all of those flies?"

While Mr. Granger was standing at the register talking, I walked over to Cabbage. He didn't have anything in his pockets. I told him to walk back over to the aisle I was on and load up, but he was too busy playing scaredy cat.

"Get out of here, Mr. Granger. Buy whatever you came in here for and get out before I call the sheriff."

"You can't put me out. Somebody around here has to know where I can get my wife some velvet." He looked at me and I shrugged my shoulders.

"Cabbage, have you found the sugar yet?" old Potter asked. "It's taking you an awfully long time."

"I'm looking for salt, too," said Cabbage.

"Well, Sonny just passed the salt. Salt is on aisle five."

"I didn't see it," I said. Old Potter cut his eyes at me and pointed his finger toward aisle five.

17.

"All right Granger, you either buy something or get the hell out of here."

"I want to buy some velvet for my wife. It's the finest piece of cloth my wife has ever seen. She wants to wear velvet just like Mrs. Wick. Sofia told me Mrs. Wick stopped wearing velvet when her boy ran away from home."

"Out, Mr. Granger. What does a man like you know about a woman of quality like Mrs. Wick. You know you shouldn't pay any attention to Sofia. She's crazy," said old Potter. I could tell that old Potter was losing his patience with Mr. Granger and I knew Cabbage needed more time loading up. I had to keep Mr. Granger talking.

"Who is Sofia, Mr. Granger?"

"Oh, everybody knows Sofia. She's Mrs. Wick's maid. Mrs. Wick doesn't get out as much since her boy ran away. Sofia does everything for her now."

"Why did her boy run away?" I asked.

"Stop egging him on, Sonny," said old Potter. "I don't have any velvet to sell to you, Mr. Granger."

"He thinks I'm not good enough to buy velvet because I work at the cotton mill. I got money to buy velvet. Look here. I'll show you." Mr. Granger sat his flask on the counter and took a small bag out of his pocket. Old Potter watched him turn the bag right side up.

"Don't you pour that money on this counter, you drunk fool." Mr. Granger turned the bag all the way over, and pennies came rushing down all over the counter. I told Cabbage to make a run for it. We ran out of old Potter's store as fast as we could.

We heard old Potter yelling. "See what you did! I knew those boys were stealing from me. I could have caught them. You see what you did, you drunk fool!" We ran deep into the woods until we got to the Oconee River. We pulled out our loot and Cabbage started playing scaredy cat again.

"Sonny, I don't think running away is good. I want to go home."

"You can't turn your back on me now. We haven't gone anywhere." Cabbage was shaking all over like all of a sudden it was winter.

"I don't want to run away. I don't want to leave home anymore." Cabbage cried and walked away from me.

"Go home then, you big baby. See what happens to you. They're going to send you to the reformatory. Just watch. And nobody's going to come to visit you."

18.

"I DON'T BLAME CABBAGE," said Cleophus. "I would have gone back home, too. He did the right thing, if you ask me." Mr. Boyer had given us two of his cigarettes and let us stand outside the library's back door for a smoke break. We could see everybody walking around the exercise yard the way chickens do when they are fenced in on a farm. I saw Squeak leaning on the fence and looking out beyond it.

"So where is Cabbage now?" Cleophus asked me.

"Cabbage ended up going to college up North; then he got into a real bad motorcar accident and died."

"It sounds like Cabbage was on the right track," said Cleophus.

"He was. Momma and Daddy couldn't stop bragging about him."

"Are your folks still living?" Cleophus asked me. He blew out smoke and it faded in the air.

"My daddy's still alive. But he doesn't bother with me much."

"Do you ever think it's funny how Cabbage ended up in college, and you ended up in the pen? Have you ever thought about why things turned out that way?"

"No. Not really."

"If I ever get out of this place, you know what I want to do? I want to go to a real library. You know, like the ones they have in colleges. I bet I'd find all kinds of books. The kind you'd never see in a place like this. I bet I'd find stacks and stacks on Indians, too. That's all I was interested in reading about when I first came here. The Indians used to own all of this land, you know. That's something worth knowing."

"I don't think that's worth knowing. They don't own it now," I said, blowing out smoke and stomping my cigarette out with my shoe.

"Well, you ought to know it. It's a part of history. There are plenty of history books in the stacks. I think I'm about the only one who ever reads them."

"I ain't got time for reading about history."

"Can you read? Some of the new fish come here ignorant as hell. They can't even read their own names on a piece of paper."

"I can read. I went to school."

"You didn't finish, did you? Most of the new fish never even finish high school." I looked at Cleophus. I was ashamed, but I wasn't about to let him know he was right about me and school. I saw how the sunlight caught part of his face and for some reason it made me think of Cabbage standing by the river. Boyer came out and told us not to forget there were some donated dictionaries in the storage, and they needed to be put out on the reference shelf. We walked in behind him and he locked the exit door. When we got back to the stacks, I told Cleophus what happened to me after Cabbage left.

19.

I WALKED ALONG the Oconee River until I saw a house I had never seen before. It sat just off a dirt road near a graveyard full of tombstones with no names on them. Walking down the road, I could see the house sitting behind a long row of pine trees that were so big they had probably been there since God was born. I walked down the narrow road that went straight up the middle of those trees until I reached the steps of the long porch with the tall columns. The house looked smaller close up than it was far back. The paint on the house was chipping. The shutters had fallen off two of the windows and one looked like it would fall at any minute and run off some of the cats sleeping in the rocking chairs on the porch. One of the windows on the second floor was open, and the curtain hung out. I kept hearing the sound of glass breaking. It seemed to me that it was coming from the room where the curtain hung out of the window. The front door was solid wood. I must have knocked until my knuckles got sore, but nobody came. Then I heard a woman scream.

20.

"EXCUSE ME! Are you all right up there?" An old lady stuck her head out of the window. The curtain was on her shoulder until she moved it out of her way. I wished you could have seen her. Her hair was sprawled all over her head like a ball of wire, and her dress hung off her shoulders. She shaded her eyes with her hands to see me better.

"Are you all right up there, miss?"

"Albert, is that you? I knew you'd come back home. I knew you'd come back," she said.

"No, miss, my name is not Albert," I told her.

"Well, have you seen him? Sofia is gone and I need Albert to help me." The woman left the window, and I heard the sound of glass breaking in the room again. It scared the cats so bad they ran past me and into the thick bushes in the yard.

"Excuse me! Are you all right up there?" She stuck her head out of the window again and shaded her eyes with her hands to see me.

"Who are you? And where's Sofia? I need her to get my tea and help me get these birds out of my room."

"My name is Sonny."

"Is that so? My name is Mrs. Wick and everybody calls me Mrs. Wick. Do you like cats?"

"I do, but I like dogs better."

"I've got ten cats, and I told Sofia to make sure they were put to bed before nine. Sofia doesn't like cats. Have you seen Sofia?"

"No. I haven't."

"She'll be back. You don't know Sofia the way I do. She'll be back. Somebody has to get my tea and help me get these birds out of my room."

"I can help you."

"Then what are you standing there for? The door is already open."

21.

IT TOOK ABOUT an hour before I got those birds out of Mrs. Wick's room. She threw her good tea cups at the birds, but she kept missing them. She fired me enough times that day to make me believe I was actually hired to work for her. There were all kinds of things that needed to be done around the place. It was just like being at home, except everything was bigger and better to look at. There was no way I could paint the whole house by myself, so I got the ladder out of the storage house and I fixed the shutters instead. Mrs. Wick fired me again for keeping up so much racket with the hammer. She told me Sofia was trying to kill her and that I could sleep in her room off the kitchen. I didn't get one bit of sleep because Mrs. Wick walked around the house moaning about Albert all night. She kept saying that Sofia was coming up the stairs, but we were the only two people in the house.

My momma always said that sometimes a little tonic went a long way. I suggested Mrs. Wick drink some from the bottle I found in the kitchen. Her mind got better when she did that. Mrs. Wick cleaned herself up for tea in the afternoon with her friend, Mrs. Cush. I wished you could have seen Mrs. Cush. She was short and round with a plain face and no lips. All the feathers sticking out of her hat and all the shiny beads on her dress reminded me of a dress Aunt Ellen wore one Christmas. While I got the serving tray ready just the way Mrs. Wick showed me, I heard her laughing in the parlor like everything Mrs. Cush said was funny.

22.

"Mrs. Wick, I can't tell you how good it is to see you all dressed up again," said Mrs. Cush.

"For a long time, I didn't have a reason to get dressed up," said Mrs. Wick.

"I must declare you look fine, real fine, indeed. I heard that awful Sofia has left you again. People are treacherous."

"I expect her to come back any day now," said Mrs. Wick.

"Well, if I were you, I wouldn't take her back," said Mrs. Cush.

I brought in the teapot on a tray with teacups that didn't match, because Mrs. Wick broke so many of them trying to kill the birds in her room.

"I don't know where my manners are today. I just plum forgot to properly introduce you. You know how my mind has been lately. Please, forgive me, why don't you."

"Sure, dear. Sure," said Mrs. Cush.

"This is Albert. He's been helping me around the house."

You wouldn't believe what I did at that very moment to bring shame to Mrs. Wick's face right in front of a woman of quality like Mrs. Cush. When Mrs. Wick told Mrs. Cush my name was Albert, my hands sweated and I dropped the entire tray. The teapot and the teacups cracked, and the tea spilled all over the rug. Mrs. Cush grabbed her chest. But Mrs. Wick didn't scold me over like Momma would have. As a matter of fact, she didn't scold me at all. She just smiled like that rug meant nothing to her.

"Albert will boil some more water for tea," said Mrs. Wick.

"He should. Good help is just so hard to find these days. How will you ever replace such a fine tea set?" asked Mrs. Cush.

"Oh, I can buy another one from Magic Jack. He's probably got plenty of them stored up somewhere."

"He's having a show tonight. You should come! We haven't seen you at the show in months," said Mrs. Cush.

"I know. I need to get out more."

"Well, I guess you haven't heard the rumors," said Mrs. Cush.

"What rumors?"

"I heard that Magic Jack is going to stop doing the show. He's selling everything and retiring to Florida. Tonight might be his last show. It's at Mr. Poke's house again."

"Tonight might be the last Magic Jack Show?" asked Mrs. Wick.

"Yes and I heard Magic Jack was robbed again."

"What a shame," said Mrs. Wick.

23.

"YEAH, WHAT A SHAME," said Cleophus. "You're telling me this crazy woman named Mrs. Wick let you live in her house and take care of things until Sofia came back? Mrs. Wick sounds like a sad case." He picked up a book from the cart and looked at the numbers on the binding.

"That's right," I told him as I reached for the book he handed me.

"Didn't Mrs. Wick say Sofia was trying to kill her? Why would she want her to come back if she thought Sofia was trying to kill her?"

"I don't know. The woman can't think right unless she drinks tonic."

"Well, how did you know tonic was what she needed?" asked Cleophus.

"I didn't. I found it in the kitchen, and I just remembered that my momma used to drink it when she wanted to feel better."

"I bet your momma was probably drinking gin or something, and you changed it to tonic to hide the fact that she was a drunk like Mr. Granger. Your daddy was probably a worse drunk than she was."

"No, he wasn't. My momma didn't drink, and my daddy never took a drink except on the holidays."

"I bet he had a whole lot of those, just like my old man. When your daddy got drunk, I bet he knocked you and your brother around a few times, too, didn't he?" asked Cleophus.

"My daddy never laid a hand on us. Do you want to hear what happened after Mrs. Cush left Mrs. Wick's house or not?" The books from the cart were finally put in the right order on the shelves. We pushed the cart to the back to get the ones Boyer had cataloged and piled on the table.

"Sure. Go right ahead. It's your story."

24.

AFTER MRS. CUSH LEFT, Mrs. Wick called me into the parlor. I was all set to run away again because I figured I would get my scolding when the company was gone. I was ready to tell Mrs. Wick that I hadn't stolen one thing out of her house, and that I wanted to thank her for letting me sleep in Sofia's room, but none of that was necessary. Mrs. Wick called me into the parlor. She walked in circles and looked me over real good. She asked me for my size and I told her that I never knew my size. I was ashamed to tell her about the second-hand clothes the women in the church choir gave Momma for me and Cabbage. Mrs. Wick told me to follow her up the stairs and into a room she had to unlock with a key. She scrambled around in the chifforobe. She pulled out some of the fanciest clothes I had ever seen and sized them up against my chest while she nodded and shook her head.

"This used to be Albert's room. It's yours now. You're Albert."

"Mrs. Wick, I'm not Albert."

"Yes, you are. You've come back home just in time for the last Magic Jack Show. That's where my husband, Culver, bought me that tea set. He died a few years ago."

"I promise I'll pay you back every dime for the tea set."

"Well, I have a better idea and it won't cost you anything."

"What is it?"

"Come with me to the Magic Jack Show tonight. You'll love it. Plus, you'll get a chance to meet Sofia. There's no telling when she's coming home." Seeing how I still felt bad for breaking the tea set, I let Mrs. Wick change me into a real fine gentleman using Albert's clothes. I wished you could have seen me. I had never had on clothes that fancy in my life. Mrs. Wick said I looked handsome. I bet my own momma wouldn't be able to recognize me, if she could have seen me all dressed up. The shoes Mrs. Wick gave me were too small. She ran into another room and came back with a pair of her husband's shoes. They fit me just fine.

25.

"Walk."

"What do you mean, Mrs. Wick?"

"Walk across the room for me."

I walked.

"You need to walk tall and pretend you own the world." I took in as much air as I could to help straighten my back until it satisfied her. I put my shoulders back the way she showed me and strutted across the room. Prancing around all fancied up didn't make me feel like myself at all. I felt like somebody else.

Mrs. Wick spent so much time trying to teach me how to be a fine gentleman there was only time for her to swallow a little of that tonic and grab her pocketbook before we left to go to Mr. Poke's house. I wished you could have seen Mr. Poke all dressed up in a tuxedo. He was a tall man, and he walked with a cane that had a bunch of fancy carvings on it. Mrs. Wick told me he was a widower, and he sent his son off to a fancy boarding school after his wife died.

His house wasn't that much bigger than Mrs. Wick's house, but it was something every human being should see once before leaving the earth. Mr. Poke had large paintings in the hallway of people who stared at you long and hard like they could see into your soul. Chairs were set up in the parlor. In front of them sat a long table covered with a shiny cloth. There were things under the cloth, but nobody could tell exactly what they were. As more folks walked into the room in fancy clothes and hats, a skinny woman wearing a head scarf stepped out of the closet. She blew out two candles and stepped back into the closet. She giggled as she closed the door behind her.

26.

MRS. CUSH WALKED IN holding the arm of a man. Mrs. Wick said he was her husband, Mr. Cush. I wished you could have seen Mr. Cush with his long moustache twisted up on both ends. He checked his pocket watch and looked around the room. He shook his head like he had seen better places. Mrs. Cush wore a different hat. It had more feathers in it than the one I saw her in before. She complained about the heat until Mr. Cush told her to shut up.

"Where have my manners been, Mr. Cush? I just plum forgot to properly introduce you. You know how my mind has been lately. Please, forgive me, why don't you."

"Sure, Mrs. Wick, sure. I'm glad to see you out again," said Mr. Cush.

"Mr. Cush, this is Albert. He has been helping me out around the house."

"That terrible Sofia left again," said Mrs. Cush.

"Nice to meet you, Albert." Mr. Cush shook my hand. I wished you could have seen how nervous I was. My hands sweated. If I had a tray, I would have dropped it.

"Oh look, there's that awful Sofia over there blowing out the rest of the candles. We still have two minutes before the show starts, and she is already blowing out all of the candles," said Mrs. Cush, fanning herself with her hand. "That Sofia has no shame. People just don't know loyalty anymore." Sofia blew out the last candle, then sat down in one of the chairs in the front row.

"Shut up," said Mr. Cush, checking his pocket watch. "Sofia blew out the candles because the show is about to start." We sat in chairs that were closest to the window because Mr. Cush said his wife would need air if she decided to faint at half past the hour.

Magic Jack walked into the room. He wore a tuxedo with a cape, a top hat, gloves, and he had on an eye mask. I wished you could have seen him. Everybody stood up and clapped their hands, and he bowed. He snatched the cloth off the table. Under the cloth was some of the finest merchandise I had ever seen in my life. I saw everything from a shiny shotgun to a walking cane that looked even fancier than the one Mr. Poke had. Standing in the middle of everything was a whole tea set. I pointed it out to Mrs. Wick. She looked at it and smiled.

27.

"I DIDN'T FEEL so bad once I saw Mrs. Wick smile," I told Cleophus. He looked at me long and hard.

"Who taught you how to play this game?" he asked me.

"What game?"

"I've been a prisoner a long time, and I know the game you're playing. It takes most new fish at least a year to learn it, and even longer to become good at it. Somebody's been teaching you. I can tell. You can't fool me. You think you can, but you can't. I can see right through you."

"I'm not trying to fool anybody. I'm just telling you a story. It's probably the best story you ever heard in this hellhole."

"Stay around here for a while and you'll hear plenty of stories. Everybody around here has a story. Half of them don't have a spark of truth in them. But then again, that doesn't matter much when you're locked up in prison."

"Are you going to let me finish telling my story or not?"

"Sure. Go right ahead and play God if you want to."

28.

ONE BY ONE, Magic Jack took off his gloves, his cape, and his top hat and handed them to Sofia. Sofia giggled while everybody watched her fold the cape. Sofia pushed it down into the top hat along with the gloves.

"The first thing up for bid is this fine velvet cloth. We will start the bidding at five hundred dollars. Do I hear more?" asked Magic Jack.

"Five hundred dollars!" said Mr. Poke. Everybody looked at him.

Mr. Cush tried to keep his wife from raising her hand, but it didn't work. "Six hundred dollars!" said Mrs. Cush.

"Six hundred and fifty dollars!" shouted Sofia. Then she covered her mouth with her hand like her bid had slipped out by accident.

"Six hundred and fifty dollars for this fine velvet cloth. Do I hear more?"

I heard someone in the back of the room say, "Eight hundred dollars."

"Nine hundred dollars," said Sofia.

"Oh, I can't stand the thought of seeing that awful Sofia walking around Moon County wearing velvet," said Mrs. Cush.

"Sofia doesn't have that kind of money and you know it. No woman in her right mind would spend that kind of money on velvet cloth. That's too much for velvet," said Mr. Cush. "You already have dresses made out of velvet."

"Well, I want to have another one made new! One thousand dollars!" said Mrs. Cush.

"One thousand dollars for this fine velvet cloth. Going once."

"We don't want that, Jack! We give back the bid," said Mr. Cush. He stood up and shook his finger.

"Going twice!"

"I want that velvet cloth!" hollered Mrs. Cush.

"Didn't you hear me, Jack? One thousand dollars is too much for velvet. You know that. You make us pay too much!"

"Mr. Cush, that's the amount your wife called. Sooooold for one thousand dollars to the lady wearing the hat in the second row!" Nothing stopped Mrs. Cush from walking up to Magic Jack to pay for that velvet cloth. She had more cash in her hand than I had ever seen in my life.

"You'll be a wise man, Albert, not to marry a woman who likes velvet," said Mr. Cush.

"Good night, Mrs. Wick, we will be going home now. I have had about enough of this foolishness." Mr. Cush grabbed his wife and pushed her out of the parlor. Magic Jack moved on to the next item.

29.

"WE WILL START the bidding for this fine tea set at five hundred dollars. Do I hear five hundred?"

"Five hundred dollars," said a woman from the back row.

"Going once!"

"Six hundred dollars," said Mrs. Wick.

"Seven hundred dollars," hollered the man sitting behind us.

"Eight hundred dollars," said Sofia.

Mrs. Wick stood up and looked around at the crowd. "One thousand dollars," she said. The room got so quiet I could hear my own heart beat.

"Going once. Going twice! Sooooold for one thousand dollars to the woman standing up in the second row."

Sofia walked over to Mrs. Wick and gave her a hug and a kiss. Everybody in the room stood up and clapped for Mrs. Wick; then everybody started to clap louder and shouted for Magic Jack to take off his eye mask. Magic Jack removed it. I wished you could have seen who was behind that mask. It was old Potter. I ran. Just before I could get out the door, old Potter grabbed me, and he wouldn't let me go. He told everybody that I robbed him, and the crowd booed. I thought Mrs. Wick would put in a good word for me, but she told the crowd that she didn't know who I was. I figured the tonic must have worn off. Old Potter grabbed me by the collar of Albert's shirt and dragged me to that closet Sofia had hidden in earlier and he locked me in there until he finished the auction. When the auction was over, he took me to the sheriff and they shipped me off to prison. One minute, I was sitting with the finest people in Moon County, and the next minute I was sitting in the pen in Sparta County with the worst.

30.

"LIFE IS LIKE THAT," said Cleophus, "but you know good and well you don't get sent to prison for stealing candy bars from a grocery store. But nothing kills a good story like the truth."

We sorted the last of the books on the cart before our work detail was over. We told Boyer we would get to the dictionaries in the storage first thing the next morning. Boyer waited with us until Briggs came and walked us down to the dining hall. All of the voices hit us like a loud roar when we opened the doors. We got our food and sat down to eat at a corner table where it wasn't as noisy. I felt everybody's eyes on me, but I didn't stare back. That was one thing Cleophus told me not to do. I just followed him and I sat where he sat. Cleophus said that nobody would bother me as long as he was around. After we ate, he walked me back to my cell and told me he would come back and walk with me to the shower if I wanted him to. I wasn't ready to shower. He told me he would come back later and walk me to the dining hall for dinner.

After Cleophus left, I laid in my bunk waiting for Squeak. I was a little worried about him because I hadn't seen him since that morning. It was ten minutes till four and Briggs would be coming around to do the count, but there was still no sign of Squeak. Briggs came by with his clipboard. I told him that I hadn't seen Squeak. He said he didn't know Squeak was locked up with his daddy. The next day the guards wouldn't let anybody out of the cells after the morning count. There was chatter going up and down the cellblock. When the news got to me, I felt something sink in my stomach. Squeak was found dead in one of the bins in the laundry room. Some of the men started cheering and calling out my name. All I could do was put the pillow over my head and pretend that I was somewhere else.

31.

THE NEXT DAY, Boyer gave Cleophus the keys to the storage. He opened it and I walked in. The storage was cold and it had a musty odor. I walked in first; Cleophus came behind me and closed the door. He flipped on the light switch. The storage was really a long closet with boxes and books stacked on each side. Cleophus searched for the dictionaries on one side, and I searched on the other side. Then he fell over on me and I went down. I got up, but he stayed down holding his back. Beside him was a roll of money that must have fallen out of his pocket.

"Where did you get all of that money?" I asked him.

"Booker finally paid me the money he owed me. I'm going to buy myself a glass eye. How do you think I'll look?"

"I don't know. We better find those dictionaries and get out of here."

"There they are right there. I tripped over one of them."

I looked where Cleophus pointed, but I could see that all of the dictionaries were stacked real neat next to a stack of boxes.

"You're going to have to help me get up. I think I might have pulled something in my back. I've had problems with my back since I started sleeping on prison bunks." I helped him get to his feet. "Can you squeeze right here for me?" He touched the lower part of his back. "Just a touch here and there should do the trick," he said.

"I'm not your nurse, you old bastard. You need to go to the infirmary or Mann Ann if you want somebody to touch you. I've got work to do." I went to the door to bring in the cart so I could load the books. Cleophus laughed and stretched his arms over his head. We loaded the dictionaries on the cart and pushed it out to the reference shelf.

"Are you mad at me?" asked Cleophus.

"No. I'm not mad, but I'm not stupid either. I knew you fell on purpose. Those dictionaries weren't in your way."

"You're smarter than I thought you were. I guess I'll have to get up a little earlier in the morning if I want to fool old Sonny, right?"

"That's right. I'm not Squeak." He handed me a dictionary, and I put it on the reference shelf.

"Good. You know accidents happen in this place every day. The next thing you know, somebody is dead. You know why nobody makes a big fuss when somebody dies in prison?" asked Cleophus.

"Why?"

"People don't think you're a real human being once you get locked up. I could die tomorrow, and nobody would really notice I was gone. I'd just be one more sad case."

"I'd notice," I told him. "There'd be one less old bastard around here asking for back rubs."

"In a few days, you'll forget that ever happened," said Cleophus.

"Why did you pick me to work in the library with you?" I asked him.

"What do you mean?"

"You knew as well as I did what was going to happen to Squeak. Why did you save me instead of him?"

"Who says that you are saved?"

"I say so. I'm still alive and Squeak is dead, and nobody seems to care about it around here but me."

"Now, if you believe that, maybe you're not as smart as I think you are. You've got plenty of criminals around here who think they're in the insurance business. They care about the dead more than you'll ever know. They are all around you, and they look you over every day. You can't see them because you're a new fish."

"Why did you pick me instead of Squeak?"

"I picked you because I could tell you were a lot smarter than he was."

"How could you know something like that? I might be the one who tries to kill you."

"I can look at you and tell you couldn't kill anybody. I might have one eye, but I feel like I can see with four of them. I've felt this way since I lost my eye in a prison fight a long time ago. I've always believed that fight cost me my chance at parole."

"When are you up for your next parole hearing?"

"In a year or two, but they will never give me parole. I'll have to take my forty-five years all the way to the door. I've got fifteen more to go, and that's a long time. It doesn't bother me much. When I got here, I knew I was going to die here. The world started preparing me to come to prison the day I was born."

"How did you end up in here?"

"I stabbed my Uncle Ray. I was around your age when I did it. When I saw you that day in your cell, it was like seeing myself behind bars all over again. That was a hard pill for me to swallow."

"So you got forty-five years for stabbing a man?"

"I got forty-five years because I stabbed him and he died."

"Why did you stab him?"

"I had to kill him or he was going to kill me. That's the law I had to live by growing up. I must admit it felt good killing that mean bastard. It gave my mind a rush. You don't get rushes like that except when you are with a woman, and you don't see too many of them in places like this."

"You mean you are glad you killed him?"

"Do you want me to answer with the truth, or do you want me to play that game you were playing?" asked Cleophus.

"I don't care what you do," I told him.

"You should, but every man has to make his own choices. You know, I've been known to tell a pretty good story myself. Anytime you tell a story, you'd better make sure you don't end up being the fool in it."

"I know. The trick is learning what kind of stories to tell, and who to tell them to."

"That trick doesn't always work. Sometimes, it doesn't matter what kind of story you tell or who you tell it to. A story is about more than just the story."

32.

THAT WAS CLEOPHUS for you, always laying down a proverb when all I wanted him to do was tell me why he killed his uncle. I had to admit that Cleophus was right about me and killing. I could never do it. I always wanted to know folks who did do it. I knew an old murderer like Cleophus was more than happy to tell me everything I wanted to know. We went to the back of the library and loaded the piles of books on the cart that Boyer had put in order for us. We headed to the stacks. Cleophus stood on the ladder while I handed him books from the cart. I asked him again why he killed his uncle. I felt like Cleophus didn't want to answer the question. I told him I thought it was strange how he clammed up when the shoe was on the other foot, and somebody else was asking all the questions. Cleophus told me he wasn't clammed up at all.

"Then why won't you answer the question I asked you about your Uncle Ray?"

"I needed some time to think about it. The answer ain't as simple as you think it is. The problem started long before Uncle Ray. I used to walk around carrying a knife, so I was bound to end up killing somebody."

"What kind of knife did you have?" I asked him.

"It was a special knife given to me by a half-Cherokee Indian named Hawkeye," Cleophus said.

"What was so special about the knife?"

"It was supposed to protect me."

"Who was it supposed to protect you from, your Uncle Ray?" I asked him.

"Now that I think about it, I guess that's what that knife was for. It's a long story," he said.

"Well, you might as well tell it, seeing how neither one of us is going anywhere anytime soon," I said.

"You're right about that." Cleophus cleared his throat and told me the story about his Uncle Ray.

33.

I TOOK A WHOLE lot of beatings from my Uncle Ray, and plenty more from my daddy. Uncle Ray was my daddy's oldest brother, and he owned a farm. My daddy was a sharecropper. You almost wouldn't believe the two of them were brothers, because they hardly ever spoke to one another. They were two of the saddest cases I'd ever seen in my life. Daddy went to his grave working on Mr. Angel's land and hoping one day he could be like Uncle Ray. Mr. Angel owned almost everything we had, even the little shack we lived in. We had to give him almost all of the cotton we grew. Mr. Angel said Daddy was the best farmer he had, but you could never tell that by the pay Mr. Angel gave him. Sometimes, we could see Mr. Angel sitting up on the hill in his old truck, smoking his cigar and watching us work in the hot sun. Daddy told me to pretend like he wasn't there and keep driving the mule, but I couldn't. I always felt his eyes on the two of us as we moved up and down the field sweating in the heat like pigs. One day, Mr. Angel walked down to the field dressed up in his Sunday suit and hat. He stood next to my daddy, who wore nothing but his sweat and a pair of worn pants. I hardly ever saw my daddy smile, but he did that day. Mr. Angel took off his hat and wiped his sweaty head with his handkerchief.

"What's your secret?" he asked Daddy.

"Ain't no secret at all, boss," Daddy said. He always called Mr. Angel boss.

"Well, how come your crops grow bigger and better than anybody else's around here?" Mr. Angel asked. He tilted his head to the side and blew smoke out of his mouth.

"Just hard work, boss. Just hard work. Like you tell me all the time, work hard and one day this land is going to be mine."

"You think you might have a better cotton crop this year than last?"

"Yes sir. Sure do. Guaranteed. I'll be finished working down my debt too. You told me I owed twenty-five more dollars. This crop will bring in way more than that, so I reckon I should have a profit this time. Right boss? My wife needs some cloth to make clothes for my boys and maybe a dress for herself."

"Well, you know planting season is always expensive. Plus, you got to buy cotton seed from me and that ain't ever cheap."

"There should be plenty profit left over," I said. Daddy looked at me and frowned.

"Lucky, that boy of yours has sure grown up to be a man who ain't short on words. How old are you now, Cleophus?" Mr. Angel asked me.

"Seventeen," I told him.

"He knows how things are, right?" Mr. Angel asked Daddy. He put his cigar in his mouth and pressed his lips together.

"He knows, boss."

"Good. Remember, planting season is always more expensive than anybody can ever predict. We'll just have to see how things turn out when the time comes." Mr. Angel patted Daddy on his shoulder and winked at me. He marched back to his truck. When the truck was out of sight, my daddy turned to me and slapped me across my face with the back of his hand. I landed on the ground on my back. I didn't move. He stepped over me and walked over to the mule. I just laid in the field staring at the sun and wondering how much longer I was going to be able to stay alive.

34.

"DID YOUR DADDY hit you for speaking out of turn in front of Mr. Angel?" I asked Cleophus as he flipped through the book I handed to him.

"No, he hit me for telling the truth in front of Mr. Angel. Back then, everything was backwards and right was wrong and wrong was right. Even though my daddy knew Mr. Angel was cheating him, he always had to pretend he wasn't."

"Why didn't he just go to the sheriff?" I asked.

"The sheriff, and pretty much everybody else, was on Mr. Angel's side. My daddy didn't stand a chance against Mr. Angel.

All he could do was drink gin and tell us stories about what he was going to do when that land became his."

"Did Mr. Angel ever give him the land?"

"Hell no! Nobody ever gives you anything in this world. I used to think Daddy was a damn fool for believing Mr. Angel, but the older I got, the more I realized this was the only thing he had left to believe in. Even if it was a lie, it kept him going."

"What about your Uncle Ray?" I asked him.

"I'll get to him after I finish telling you about my daddy. He was the reason me and my brother Joe Henry ended up living with my Uncle Ray in the first place," said Cleophus.

35.

My daddy worked that land from sunup until sundown, trying to make the best out of a bad situation. When chores around the house were finished, Momma would come out and help us in the field. She was a small woman with a sweet face, but she could work long and hard like a man. She couldn't read and neither could my daddy. Daddy let me go to school long enough to get at least half a notion on how to figure out Mr. Angel's calculations, and how to read enough to make out the print in the newspaper. I didn't get much of an education until I got to prison. Momma talked Daddy into letting my younger brother Joe Henry stay in school because he was sick all the time. Because of all the dust in the field, he wasn't of much use when he was out there. When his eyes weren't running, he was sniffing, and when he wasn't sniffing, he was coughing. Joe Henry was a sad case. Sometimes, Daddy would sit on the porch with a bottle of gin and just stare at him and shake his head. I don't think he saw me in a light that was much better. He probably looked at us and saw something worse than he saw in himself. I think he wanted to change the way things were, but he couldn't, and that made him one mean bastard.

He started to change a little when he met Hawkeye. Daddy was the one who told me Hawkeye was half-Cherokee Indian, but nobody knew exactly where he came from or where he lived.

He was always walking around Moon County, looking and inspecting like everybody was doing everything the wrong way. Then one day, Daddy pulled up in the wagon with Hawkeye. Hawkeye had deep-set eyes, and he always wore a hat with chicken feathers sticking out of the back. His clothes were dirty and full of holes. He told Daddy that he knew how to make cotton grow, and Daddy believed him. He let Hawkeye bless the land right before planting season. He stood out in the field and raised his hands. He mumbled words we didn't understand; and then he started singing. That year we had one of the best crops ever. Mr. Angel couldn't stop saying good things about Daddy, and Daddy couldn't stop saying good things about Hawkeye. He always made Momma give Hawkeye food because we didn't have anything else to give him.

One time, Momma had gone into the house to put some food in a shoe box for him. I came up the back stairs; she didn't know I followed her. I stood in the doorway. I saw her standing with her face in a corner. Her feet were bare and dusty. I couldn't tell if she was praying, or crying, or both. I walked over to her and touched her on her shoulder. I scared her, and she tried to hide what was in her hand behind her back. I reached behind her. She didn't put up much of a fight like I expected her to. In her hand, there was a little cross she had made out of two sticks and thread. I told her everything was going to be all right. Momma said we hardly had enough food for ourselves and that she didn't think Hawkeye's blessings did us any good. I told her that Hawkeye's blessings were helping a lot. She shook her head. She said all that talk about Hawkeye's blessings was superstition and that we needed Jesus. I told her that I believed Hawkeye. She shook her head and handed me Hawkeye's food. I went looking for Hawkeye. I found him sitting out by the Oconee River shaving a stick with a knife.

36.

"MY DADDY WANTS *you to come bless his land,*" I told him.

"*I know. I heard his thoughts in the wind. I keep telling him that it ain't his land,*" Hawkeye said. *He looked up at the sun;*

then he took a scoop of dirt in his hand and poured it out like water.

"I know. It's Mr. Angel's land."

"It ain't Mr. Angel's land either. No man can ever own land. It owns man. All the seasons are buried there. All of the Gods are buried there, too. I've told your daddy this. He doesn't listen. He doesn't hear. He hears only what he wants to hear. I told him the end is coming. He didn't believe me."

"What end are you talking about?" I asked him.

"The end to everything is coming. You better be careful. I see danger for you and your daddy. Tell your daddy I can't bless the land. Tell him there is nothing I can do to help him anymore."

"He's going to want to know why."

"Tell him that the end is coming. Men die. Land lives forever. Tell him he will never own that land no matter how hard he works. I told him he should leave, but he doesn't listen. Now, it is too late."

I walked away, and when I turned around, Hawkeye was gone.

37.

"You mean Hawkeye just disappeared?" I asked as I handed him another book to place on the shelf.

"Yeah. I turned around and he was gone. I was walking less than a minute."

"Are you trying to say he was a ghost?"

"I'm just telling you what I saw. I turned around and the man was gone," said Cleophus.

"That's a ghost. One minute it's there and the next minute it ain't."

"Well, that was Hawkeye for you. Sometimes he was around, and sometimes he wasn't. I can't say that he was a ghost because I don't know."

"I bet your daddy got mad when you told him."

"He sure did. I'll never forget the look on his face when I told him," said Cleophus.

38.

AFTER I TOLD my daddy what Hawkeye told me to tell him, he said that Hawkeye was crazy. Daddy said that if Hawkeye didn't want to bless the land anymore, then he could go to hell. Daddy told Momma to bring the Bible out of the house. He held it up in the sky and blessed the land himself. We noticed later that our cotton crop wasn't growing like it had before.

We took the little we could gather up to Mr. Angel's barn. Mr. Angel didn't even weigh it. He just took all of what we had and charged daddy for a loss instead of a profit. He told Daddy that if he ever wanted to own the land, then he had better turn his cotton crop around, and turn it around quick. I told Mr. Angel that Hawkeye said nobody would ever own the land. Daddy and Mr. Angel stared at me for a long time. Mr. Angel walked away from us laughing. All the way back to the house, Daddy didn't say a word to me. I knew what he was going do to me when we got home. I thought I was going to die that day.

Momma stood on the porch watching us come down the dusty road. She shook her head as Daddy marched past the house and I lagged behind him with my head down. Joe Henry tried to stop me, but Daddy told him to let me go. I followed him all the way out to the tree near the edge of the field. I turned around and saw momma and Joe Henry shading their eyes so they could see. Daddy stood under the tree waiting for me. He balled his fist. I could hear him breathing hard. He waved me closer to him with one of his hands. I walked closer to him. I felt like something hot had rolled down my back. He waved me closer. I got close enough to smell him. I looked down at his worn boots with wire for laces. He lifted my head. Just when I could see my reflection in his eyes, one of his fists caught me on my jaw, and I stepped back to catch my balance. Before I could straighten myself up, Daddy punched me in my stomach, and I fell on my knees.

"Get up, Cleophus! You look like a man. You talk like a man. I want to see if you can fight like a man. Get up!"

I was slow getting to my feet. There was a part of me that knew I had to fight him or I would die. I didn't want to, but I knew I had too. Daddy let me get up. I grabbed him around his waist and he locked his arms around my head. We fell on the ground. He pushed me off of him and jumped to his feet. He grabbed me by the neck of my shirt and pulled me up. We stood toe to toe. I felt his breath on my skin.

"Hawkeye said that you are never going to own this land no matter how hard you work. This land won't ever be yours. He said that we should leave," I said.

"You and Hawkeye can both go to hell. I see the way you perk up when he comes around. I hear you repeating his sayings to your momma. You think he's better than me, don't you?"

"No," I told him and that was the truth.

"You'll tell me anything. You get a little growth on you and you think you're a man. But I know what you are. You're a fucking no account, that's what you are. You're a goddamn troublemaker, too!" Daddy swung wide and his fist landed on my mouth. I felt my lip swelling. He socked me in my right eye and I fell on my back. Daddy jumped down on me and grabbed my neck. He choked me. All I could do was grab his arms and kick my legs. I felt my right eye swelling shut. Tears fell out of Daddy's eyes and landed on my face. If it wasn't for Joe Henry, I don't think I'd be alive today.

39.

"What did Joe Henry do, Cleophus? Did he kill him?" I asked.

"No. It wasn't in Joe Henry's nature to kill. He couldn't even kill chickens and rabbits."

"So, how did he save you?"

"Joe Henry must have grabbed one of the shovels standing against the side of the house that day. He swung it and hit Daddy in the head. You'd think the boy had been swinging shovels his whole life the way blood ran down Daddy's face. When Joe Henry helped me get to my feet, I kept walking toward the road. I didn't look back. I didn't know where I was going, but I walked as far away from that house as I could."

"I bet Joe Henry tried to go, too."

"Yeah, he begged me to take him with me, but I told him to go back. He was better off staying with Momma."

"Where did you end up going?" I asked Cleophus.

"I was going any place I could go. Then, I heard somebody calling my name and I turned around," he said.

"It was Hawkeye, wasn't it?"

"It sure was."

"What did he want?"

"He came to tell me that my daddy was going to be dead before sundown."

"What did you do?" I asked.

"I did the only thing I could do. I ran away with Hawkeye," said Cleophus.

40.

I FOLLOWED HAWKEYE deep into the backwoods until we came to a spot cleared for a fire. He sat me down, took a leaf from his pocket, and told me to hold it over my swollen eye. He struck two rocks together and started a fire. We stood up and looked down into the flames. Hawkeye told me to stare at them until I saw the sun, the stars, and the clouds. I told him I saw them, but I really didn't see anything at all. He took off his hat and we sat down.

"The danger for you and your daddy is near, and there is nothing either one of you can do to stop it from coming," Hawkeye said.

"What danger? What is going to happen to us?" I asked Hawkeye.

"Somebody will kill your daddy and somebody will take one of your eyes, but you will see with four of them," he told me.

"How do you know what is going to happen to my eye?" I asked him.

"I saw it in the fire. The gods of the land have spoken."

"What kind of gods are you talking about?"

"The ones buried in the land we're sitting on right now. They are the beginning and the end," Hawkeye said.

"Ask them to help me."

"They already have. You are still alive. They have protected you for a long time, but they see your manhood waiting for you over the horizon. You have to go back home and claim it. I can't tell you how to do that, but I can tell you the story of the gods."

41.

RIGHT THERE by the fire, Hawkeye told me the story about the gods who had been keeping me alive that whole time. I know that story like the back of my hand. I can tell it just as good as Hawkeye could.

He told me that first, it was dark. Summer God came from above the sun, stars, and clouds. Winter God came from below the dirt and rocks. Spring God came from the East and Fall God came from the West. The gods married and that was how we got the earth.

Summer God said, "Sun, shine your light." The sun shined its light on the earth.

Spring God, Fall God, and Winter God were happy.

Spring God said, "I have come to bring life." Spring God called the earth and the sun, and together they created Standing Bear. Winter God whispered his name in his ear.

Fall God said, "I have come to take you to your wife." Fall God took Standing Bear to the West for four days and returned with a woman. Summer God whispered her name in her ear. He called her Singing Wind.

Winter God, Summer God, Spring God, and Fall God were happy.

Then there was a four-year war fought between Summer God and Winter God because somebody had stolen Singing Wind away from Standing Bear. He roamed the earth trying to find her. Spring God and Fall God searched the earth to find Singing Wind. They searched under the dirt and rocks. She was not there. They searched above the clouds, stars, and sun. They *found her sitting on a mountain with a knife in her hand. She sang a song.*

Winter God caused angry winds to blow dirt into Singing Wind's eyes, and he stole Standing Bear. Singing Wind cried. Summer God was angry and made it rain for four days to bring Standing Bear back to Singing Wind, but the earth flooded. Singing Wind was buried alive in the side of a mountain by Fall God, so that she would not drown.

Spring God and Fall God heard her crying. They searched the earth to find Standing Bear. They searched above the sun, stars, and clouds. He was not there. They searched under the dirt and rocks. They finally found Standing Bear sitting in a tree with a bow and arrow in his hand. Spring God moved the mountain, and brought Singing Wind out to see Standing Bear and the flooded earth. Singing Wind and Standing Bear were very sad when they saw what had happened to the earth. Summer God and Winter God were sad. Fall God and Spring God were sad. They decided to create more land to divide the flood waters into the great oceans.

42.

"WHAT KIND of story is this?" I asked. "What book did you get this story out of?"

"I didn't get this story from a book. I got it from Hawkeye. He said it was his religion."

"I have never heard of any religion like that in my life, especially not with all of those gods. It sounds like a fairytale to me."

"But it ain't. Hawkeye told me that Singing Wind and Standing Bear lived here before there ever was a place called Moon County. They were the mother and father of the land we live on. Whenever you get around to reading that book I gave you, you'll see how many people have said the same thing Hawkeye said, and he probably never read a book a day in his life," said Cleophus.

"I'm starting to think your daddy was right. Hawkeye was crazy."

"He might have been crazy, but everything he said came true. Somebody shot my daddy, and I ended up with this patch over my eye. Ever since I've been in prison, I've prayed to those gods Hawkeye told me about. I wouldn't have been able to survive this long in prison without them. What do you believe in?"

"I believe in Jesus, the Son of God," I said.

"Good. At least you believe in something. Faith is all a man has at the end of the day. I think you might want to hear the rest of what Hawkeye told me about his gods."

"I guess that's the least I can do. But I want you to know the whole thing sounds crazy to me."

"Well, just listen to the rest of the story. It won't take long," said Cleophus.

43.

HAWKEYE TOLD ME *that after the oceans were created, Fall God and Spring God decided that Summer God and Winter God could no longer be trusted together. So Fall God stood beside Summer God, and Spring God stood beside Winter God. The two gods promised Standing Bear and Singing Wind that they would remain that way forever. They were never allowed to leave the earth to go above the sun, stars, and clouds, or below dirt and rock until they died. Standing Bear was happy but Singing Wind was not. She sang a sad song to the Summer God, and the Spring God heard her sad song.*

Spring God asked, "Why do you cry, Singing Wind?"

Singing Wind said, "I do not have a child."

Spring God told Summer God, and Fall God told Winter God.

After four more days of singing her sad song, Singing Wind saw Spring God coming. He gave her a seed from the earth to eat. Singing Wind ate the seed. It grew inside her.

Summer God came one day while the other gods slept, and Standing Bear bathed in one of the great oceans. Summer God heard Singing Wind's song. Summer God told her to carve the words to the song into Standing Bear's back while he slept in the night. She did.

Winter God was so angry when he awakened to see Standing Bear's blood and Singing Wind's bloody hands, he sent a man made out of snow to steal Standing Bear. Singing Wind died of loneliness.

Fall God and Spring God told Standing Bear to bury Singing Wind in the earth. He buried her. He took the knife she used to carve the words to her song in his back, and went searching for the man made of snow. Standing Bear never found him, and he killed himself with Singing Wind's knife. The gods buried him next to Singing Wind.

44.

ONCE HAWKEYE FINISHED *telling me that story, he pointed to the sun setting behind the trees. He told me that my daddy's time had come. He reached into his pocket and pulled out the knife. He handed it to me. He said that Singing Wind told him to give it to me. I started on my way home. When I turned to look back, Hawkeye was gone.*

Daddy was not there when I got home. Momma said Daddy wasn't in his right mind after Joe Henry hit him. Daddy drank half a bottle of gin and went up to Mr. Angel's house. Momma and Joe Henry said they tried to stop him, but he wouldn't listen.

Nobody heard from him for two days. He had never stayed away that long before. I remembered what Hawkeye said to me about Daddy being in danger, but I tried not to believe it, even though I knew it was true. Momma was already worried, so I didn't want to bother her by mentioning Hawkeye's name. Each day that Daddy was missing, Momma sent me out to search for him. Instead, I went to sit with Hawkeye by the river. He taught me how to shave sticks with that knife that he gave me. Hawkeye kept asking me if I wanted him to show me where Daddy's body was. I told him no. Then the sheriff came to the house and told my momma that his men had found Daddy out by the Oconee River. Somebody had shot him. Momma dropped to her knees when she heard what had happened to him. She couldn't get out of bed for two days. She kept telling us she didn't know what we were going to do, or where we were going to go. After the funeral, Momma called me and Joe Henry into her room and made us gather around her bed.

"I want you both to listen to me and listen good," Momma said. "I'm sending you both to live with your daddy's brother."

"I don't want to go live with Uncle Ray and Aunt Trudy," I said.

"Be quiet, Cleophus. This ain't the time to be proving yourself with me. Now, I've already had a talk with your Uncle Ray. He'd be more than happy to take you and Joe Henry in. He could use the extra help on his farm."

"Where are you going to go?" asked Joe Henry. He wiped the tears from his face.

"I'm going to Atlanta to live with my sister. When I find work, I'm coming back for you both."

"Why can't we go?" I asked her.

"She doesn't have enough room to take in all three of us."

"How long will it take you to find work?" I asked.

"It won't take long. There is plenty of work for me in Atlanta."

"I want to go, too," said Joe Henry.

"Come around here, Joe Henry, and give me a hug." I watched my momma hugging Joe Henry, and I thought about how long it would take for me to walk to Atlanta from Moon County. I had never been out of Moon County a day in my life. I didn't even know where Atlanta was on a map. It just seemed like it was some place better, but it was miles away from where I was.

"You're not coming back." Momma looked at me long and hard.

"Come here, Cleophus."

"No."

"Get over here, boy. Right now! You are still in your daddy's house." I walked up to the bed and she grabbed my arm. "Don't you ever let me hear you say a thing like that again. I'm still your momma. Now, go pack up your belongings. Your uncle will be coming soon."

45.

"So who shot your daddy?" I asked Cleophus.

"I don't really know, but I believe it was Mr. Angel who shot him. After Joe Henry hit him in the head with that shovel, I guess Daddy stopped believing Mr. Angel's lies, and he wanted to do something about it."

"So, did you ever see your momma again?" I asked Cleophus.

"No. I never saw her again. I knew she was going to leave and never come back before it ever happened."

"How did you know?"

"Hawkeye told me that day we sat by the fire. Momma probably made a better life for herself without us. She deserved that. Everybody deserves that. So I decided not to hate her."

"At least your Uncle Ray and Aunt Trudy took you in."

"I wish they hadn't. Aunt Trudy made pretty dresses for herself and painted her lips. I think that's about all she could do to keep from going crazy. She didn't have any children. I used to think that was the reason her eyes looked so sad all the time. She was always quiet, almost like she had given up on life. She pretty much lived a trapped life, just like my daddy."

"You make it sound like she was in a prison."

"In some ways, she was. All prisons don't necessarily have bars. Aunt Trudy couldn't even see that she was locked up. What could she do about it if she could?"

"That's probably why she was the way she was," I said.

"No, Aunt Trudy ended up that way because she was owned."

"What do you mean she was owned?" I asked.

"Let me finish with the rest of the story and you'll see exactly what I mean," said Cleophus.

46.

MY UNCLE RAY *had a big clean house with a long porch. The house sat on a hill. Sometimes, Uncle Ray would sit out on the porch holding his hands up in the air to look at them. The man had the widest hands I'd ever seen, and his fingers looked like thick sausages. He always smoked cigars. I can't look at a cigar till this day without thinking about him. Even at the breakfast table, he'd have a cigar burning. He'd look down at his pocket watch and look over at us to see if we had made it to our chairs at the kitchen table before seven o'clock. If we were late, Uncle Ray wouldn't let Aunt Trudy serve us breakfast. Sometimes, Aunt Trudy wrapped biscuits in old newspaper and buried them in the grass out by the well for us. Joe Henry went to the well more than I did.*

"Look at you. You little beggar. You're always late. There's no excuse for it with as many roosters as I have around here. Why were you late for breakfast again?"

I watched the smoke from Uncle Ray's cigar rising up into the air in a wavy line. Joe Henry's shirt was on backwards. He still had sleep in his eyes.

"I don't know, Uncle Ray," said Joe Henry.

"What in the hell do you mean, you don't know? That's something a little girl would say. Is that what you want to be— a little girl? If you're going to live in this house, you better learn how to be a man. You hear me, Joe Henry!" Uncle Ray slammed a fist down on the table and it made Joe Henry jump.

"Leave him alone!" I hollered. Uncle Ray slapped me with one of his thick hands. He slapped me so hard I fell out of my chair and felt cold.

"Nobody talks back to me in my house. You fucking beggar. You're just like your no-account daddy. I'm the boss in this house. You fucking beggar."

Blood came out of my nose and ran down into my mouth. I was able to place myself back in my chair at the table, but everybody's face looked blurred to me. Aunt Trudy started to get up, but Uncle Ray raised his fist in front of her face and she didn't move. Aunt Trudy looked at me and her eyes glazed over with water. But she didn't cry. I kept expecting tears to drop out of her eyes, but they didn't.

"Joe Henry, your breakfast is over. Come with me out to the barn. I'm going to show you what I mean when I say the word

respect. Cleophus, clean up this mess you made," said Uncle Ray. Joe Henry started shaking. He looked at my hands covering my nose and the blood seeping through my fingers. Joe Henry recognized that I couldn't help myself, let alone him. He knew he had to make some kind of peace with what he had to face. Before he walked out of the door, he touched me on my shoulder. I felt the anger in me bubble up and sink. Uncle Ray opened the door and Joe Henry walked out. It was a sad case. Joe Henry didn't stand a chance against Uncle Ray.

After that day, I carried the knife Hawkeye gave me everywhere I went. I just didn't feel safe without it.

47.

"So, what did Aunt Trudy do when he left?" I asked.

"She got up and she took all of the dishes off the table; then she came over with a wet dish towel and wiped my face and hands and arms."

"Did she say anything?"

"Not one word, but she was talking to me with her hands," said Cleophus.

"What do you mean?" I asked him.

"After she cleaned my face, she kept looking at me. She kept rubbing my head. Then she started crying. The whole time I could hear Joe Henry screaming off in the distance. I didn't know if Aunt Trudy was crying for herself or for Joe Henry, or for all of us."

"But I bet you liked her touching you. Didn't you?"

"I did. No woman had ever touched me like that before. But I kept hearing Joe Henry scream, so I felt a little joy and a little pain all at the same time. I knew Aunt Trudy heard the screams, too, but I guess she blocked them out of her mind by pretending what was happening to Joe Henry really wasn't happening at all."

"What did Uncle Ray do to Joe Henry in the barn?"

"Uncle Ray beat him within a quarter inch of his life," Cleophus said. "We had to take Joe Henry all the way to Sparta County to get him some help because, in those days, none of the doctors in Moon County would treat him. Uncle Ray made me and Aunt Trudy lie to the doctor and say that Joe Henry fell. The doctor was young, but he wasn't a fool. He knew a good old fashion beating when he saw one. He was the one who made sure Joe Henry didn't have to come back to Moon County. One of the nurses who took care of Joe Henry took him in. They moved up North somewhere. I never saw Joe Henry again."

"I bet you wished she had taken you?"

"I did, but I knew I was too old. Nobody wanted to take in a smart talking teenager anyway. I think people looked at me and saw trouble."

"How much longer did you live with Aunt Trudy and Uncle Ray?"

"I lived with them a little while longer. Every chance she could get, Aunt Trudy was touching on me. Finally, one day we did business. Uncle Ray wasn't at home that day."

"Cleophus, you're some dirty bastard. She was your aunt."

"Maybe so, but it was my due. Uncle Ray was the reason Joe Henry was taken away from me, so I took his wife away from him. Then one day, I took him. That was the day that I became a man."

"You killed him?"

"I sure did. He caught Aunt Trudy kissing me. He slapped her and she fell to the floor. He threw me across the kitchen table and started kicking me. I reached into my pocket and grabbed the knife Hawkeye gave me, and I stabbed him in the leg. He fell and I jumped on him and stabbed him in the chest. I kept stabbing until Aunt Trudy pushed me off him. She dropped down beside him and put his head in her lap. She started rubbing it the way she rubbed mine. She kept screaming that I had killed her husband. I saw all of the blood pouring out of him. I ran. I ran fast and hard."

"Where did you go?"

"I came to Sparta County thinking I could track down Joe Henry, but I found Janie instead."

"Who's Janie?" I asked.

"She's just a girl I met. I'll tell you about the night that I first saw her sitting in that restaurant," said Cleophus.

48.

I WAS COLD and hungry by the time I got to Sparta County, so I took my chances and walked into this little restaurant on the other side of the train track. Janie was sitting by herself. I looked over at her and she looked over at me. She was made up like she was waiting for somebody to take her out and show her a good time. I don't know what made her come over and sit next to me on the barstool. She didn't even know me. Her eyes looked tired, like she needed a good night's sleep. She probably thought the same thing about me. For a long time, we just sat next to one another, not saying a word, while a short fat man behind the counter leaned on the register and listened to the radio.

"What's keeping you out so late? Your momma is probably worrying her head off," Janie said. Her voice sounded sweet.

"I don't have a momma anymore," I told her.

"What happened to her? She die?"

"She left. She went to live with her sister in Atlanta."

"Why didn't you go with her?"

"They didn't have enough room. She said she would send for me, but she never did."

"I understand. Willy went off to learn how to fly airplanes. He said he was coming back, but I haven't seen him."

"Is that your husband?" I asked her.

"No. I'm not the kind of woman men like to marry, but one day, somebody much better than Willy is going to walk through the door and take me to the altar."

"Is that why you're out so late?"

"I come here all the time to keep Fat Bobby company. Ain't that right, Fat Bobby?" she asked.

Fat Bobby looked up. "Yeah, Janie keeps me company until a man walks through the door. But I guess that's a lot better than spending every night listening to the radio news. It's always about something bad. A man was killed in Moon County yesterday. And somebody will be killed tomorrow and the next day. Pretty soon we'll all be dead," said Fat Bobby.

"Well, nobody's forcing you to listen to that radio," said Janie.

"You're not scared of what might happen to you around here?" I asked. An old man wearing a hat walked in, and he sat in front of Fat Bobby. He placed an order and Fat Bobby walked into the kitchen. We could hear him banging the pans.

"I'm not scared of anything. You smoke?" She reached into her pocketbook and pulled out a cigarette.

"Yeah." I had never touched a cigarette in my life, but I saw Uncle Ray smoking cigars all the time, and I thought that was something every man knew how to do. Janie handed me a cigarette and lit it while I held it between my lips. I drew in smoke and almost choked to death.

She patted my back. "You sure you smoke?"

"Yeah. I just had a little something in my throat."

"Where do you live around here? I've never seen you before. I would have remembered you if I did." I couldn't answer. I just looked at her. I think she could tell I was making up some lie in my head.

"I just got here. I haven't had a chance to find a place yet."

"Well, where are you going to sleep tonight?" she asked.

"I don't know. Maybe, I could stay the night at your house since Willy is gone."

"Maybe, you can. It depends on how much money you got."

"I've got a little money," I told her.

"What's your name?"

"Cleophus."

"I like that name. It sounds like a name a woman can trust." Janie reached over and kissed me; then she put her hands on my crotch. The only woman I had ever kissed like that was Aunt Trudy, but Janie's kiss was different.

49.

"WERE YOU IN LOVE with Janie?" I asked Cleophus.

"No. That wasn't love. It was just business. I can tell you don't know the difference. It's probably because you're still ripe."

"I'm not ripe. I've been with a lot of women," I told Cleophus.

"You're too young to have been with a lot of women." Cleophus grinned. "Even if you have been with a lot of women, I bet none of them were like Janie."

"I had a girl before I got locked up. Her name was Daisy."

"Where is she?"

"She died."

"It's too bad she's dead and you're locked up. In prison, there are only two ways you can get the kind of rush Janie gave me that night. You either get with another man or you kill him. It's all part of the same emotion," said Cleophus.

"What does that have to do with killing somebody?"

"When there is no love, people kill. Nobody has any reason to love anybody else unless they find one. Nobody has any reason to hate anybody else unless they find one. That's something I figured out the day they caught me."

"How did they catch you?" I asked him.

"The Moon County sheriff had been asking a lot of questions all over the place. Janie used to write me letters. In one of them, she told me that she thought Fat Bobby was the one who told the sheriff where I was. I was lying in the bed next to Janie, and we heard somebody banging on the door. I peeked out the window. They all had guns. I surrendered. I didn't want any trouble for Janie. They used the knife Hawkeye gave me for evidence and got Aunt Trudy to testify against me. I couldn't believe it. It was like seeing a different woman. She said more that day than I heard her say the whole time I lived with her. I remember the judge looked straight into my eyes when he told me he was sending me to prison for murder."

"Well, I guess everybody's got a story like that around here," I said.

"Maybe so. But ain't many folks around here with a story that ended the way mine did. There's a whole lot more you've got to hear. Three weeks after I got out of the infirmary with my eye all stitched and bandaged, the guards put a new fish in the cell with me."

"Who was he?" I asked.

"A man we called Digger. We called him that because he kept getting himself in bad situations on purpose. He was trying to die."

"What is so special about that? People do things like that all the time."

"The catch is that Digger looked just like you. I noticed it the minute I laid eyes on you. Booker noticed it too. If you don't believe me, ask Booker. He might be an old-timer, but he still remembers Digger," said Cleophus.

"Digger didn't look anything like me and you know it."

"What makes you so sure of yourself?"

"You're playing that crazy game, and you know just as well as I do that you can't play it unless you lie."

"One man's lie is another man's truth," said Cleophus.

"There you go again with those stupid proverbs. Any fool can see you're lying."

"I don't have much to lie about anymore. Those proverbs might sound stupid to you, but they sure do help to keep you honest, especially when you've been locked up in prison as long as I have. I'll never forget what happened to me when I first got here," said Cleophus.

50.

W̲H̲E̲N̲ I̲ G̲O̲T̲ H̲E̲R̲E̲, *the guards said I asked too many questions. They thought the best way to get me to shut up was to stick me in a cell in the worst cellblock there was. That's when Boaz and his boys started messing with me. Boaz had a long pointed goatee and thick eyebrows. He looked like the devil and he was always grabbing his crotch. The short chunky one was named Soupy. He didn't have any of his top front teeth. The one with the long scar down the left side of his face was named Newt. They would pass three and four times before lights out, and look me over from head to toe. They banged cups against the bars of my cell and made kissing sounds every time they passed me in the shower. I went down the cellblock line and bought a fork from a guy who worked in the kitchen. It wasn't much, but I knew I was going to need it sooner rather than later. The day came when I woke up and found the three of them standing in front of my cell. Boaz did all the talking.*

"The word around here is that you like stabbing people to death," Boaz said. I laid on the bottom bunk. I didn't move.

"That's right. What business is it of yours?" I asked him.

"Everything is my business in here, and you better get used to it," said Boaz.

"You go to hell," I told him.

"I've already been."

"Then go back and leave me the hell alone."

"I've come back for you. Starting tomorrow, you're going to be working with us in the laundry," said Boaz.

"My work detail is in the kitchen."

"Not any more. The guards tell us you ask a lot of questions. They say you need to be taken down a peg or two. When we finish with you, you're going to be just right." They hissed at me and banged their cups up against the bars as hard as they could. I didn't move. I kept thinking about Hawkeye, and praying to those gods he told me about. If the three of them had seen just how scared I was, I would have probably lost both of my eyes in that laundry room.

51.

"Dɪᴅ Bᴏᴀᴢ, Nᴇᴡᴛ, and Soupy want to rape you?" We rolled the cart around to the next aisle. Cleophus got up on the ladder and I handed him more books.

"Things like that didn't happen much back in those days. The guards were just making sure I was properly welcomed to the family. They saw Boaz, Soupy, and Newt jump me and drag me down the back hallway to the laundry room. I tried to hold them back with the fork, but that fork just couldn't hold up to the knife Boaz had. Newt and Soupy tried to corner me. Boaz came toward me with his knife. I stabbed him in the arm with the fork, and he stuck me in the eye with the knife. I must have passed out from shock or something because all I remembered was how every little noise I heard in the infirmary sounded like a bomb going off in my head. The doctor told me I'd never be able to see out of my right eye again."

"I bet you couldn't help but remember what Hawkeye told you?"

"I sure did. I told that doctor that I was told one day I would have one eye. The doctor said he was going to check my dosage to make sure that I wasn't getting too doped up."

"Whatever happened to Boaz, Newt, and Soupy?" I asked.

"Nothing," said Cleophus.

"They didn't get sent to confinement?"

"Hell no! All three of them ended up eventually getting paroled."

"How the hell did that happen?"

"Stuff like that happens all the time around here. This might be a prison, but it's a place of business. Deals are being made even as we speak. Nobody around here can be trusted," said Cleophus.

"Things in here are really no different than they are on the outside," I said.

"I'm glad to see you've figured that out. I tell the new fish that all the time. I told it to Digger about a hundred times, but he didn't listen."

"Digger is the one you said dug his own grave, right?" I asked.

"Sure did. Everybody thought he was so tough because he didn't say much. Most of us thought he would last at least a month. That's what we were betting on, but Digger didn't even last two weeks in prison. I'll tell you why," said Cleophus.

52.

AFTER I GOT OUT of the infirmary, I stayed doped up on all the pills they gave me to fight the headaches. It was confusing learning how to see with one eye; but I soon got used to it. When I did, I started seeing things differently. A lot of things I had seen before looked different when I looked at them with one eye. It changed the way I thought about things too. After I was released from the infirmary, a guard took me back to my cell. It didn't even look or feel like the same place. All the men were congratulating me and wanting to shake my hand. They told me if I ever needed anything, all I had to do was ask. Booker later told me that I had been accepted as a part of the family because I had proven I was a man. At first, the whole thing seemed backwards to me, but then I began to see what everybody else saw. My missing eye was something I was supposed to be proud of. It told everybody that I belonged.

Not long after I got out of the infirmary, the guards came marching in all the new fish. One of them was Digger. It was never good for a new fish to be thrown in with just any old convict, especially one that was as bandaged up as much as I was. When he saw me, Digger probably thought I had been fighting in a war. I stared at him. I could tell he was headed for trouble.

Digger didn't seem to have common ways about him at all. It made me think that the soil he grew up on wasn't hard. He always kept his clothes neat. He lined up all of his belongings at night before he went to bed, and he never went to sleep without brushing his teeth. When he did talk, the words came out of his mouth the way they do when the man on the radio announced the news. At first, I thought Digger thought he was better than me because he didn't listen when I told him to stop going off by himself so much. But that wasn't why he acted the way that he did. Digger acted that way because he didn't have anything to believe in. I tried to get him to read some books I checked out of the library for him. I even told him the story about Hawkeye, and the gods he told me about. Digger said he didn't believe in *any kind of god.* He said there was no such thing as God, and that he had no reason to give a damn about anything that happened in this crazy world. So, when I found out he was doing time for shooting his daddy, I didn't know what to make of it. He said he did it, but I didn't want to believe it. His daddy didn't die, but Digger said he wished he had because his life would have been better without him. I told him to lie and tell everybody in prison that his daddy died, but Digger didn't believe he needed to lie to stay alive.

Digger was a sad case. It wasn't long before somebody came banging cups against the bars. This time it was Booker, Radio, and Dill. Back then, Booker didn't wear glasses. Dill was always grinning and popping gum like he was ready for action. Radio was a half-wit with crossed eyes. Radio and Dill were released years ago. I told Digger that trouble was coming. I told him to just lie still in his bunk and not to say a word.

"How are you holding up, Cleophus?" asked Booker.

"You know, everybody is still talking about the way you stood up to Boaz. He'll be getting out of the infirmary soon, but he won't dare touch you. We're going to make sure of that. Ain't that right, Dill?" said Radio.

"That's right," said Dill, popping his gum.

"That's good to know," I said.

"We wanted to welcome Digger to the family," said Booker.

"Yeah, everybody is real glad to see you, Digger," said Dill.

"Booker's got everybody wanting to put a price on you," said Radio.

"Didn't I tell you to keep your mouth shut?" Booker slapped Radio.

"We really came here to see you, Cleophus," said Booker. He leaned on the bars of the cell. "I wanted to come by and invite you to our meeting. It's tomorrow at noon in the exercise yard. Don't be late. We like to get things started on time."

53.

"SO THE WHOLE TIME, Digger never said a word to Radio, Dill, or Booker?" I asked Cleophus.

"No. I was glad because I thought he wouldn't listen to me. He ignored the hell out of all of them just like I told him."

"Did you go to meet Booker in the exercise yard?"

"I really didn't want to leave Digger alone by himself, because I knew everybody had their eyes on him. But I was nosey. I wanted to go and see what that meeting was going to be about. I had heard a lot of talk about it, but you couldn't go if you weren't invited."

"What happened to you?" I asked holding up a book for him to place on the shelf.

"I used to think nothing happened to me; but something did happen to me on that hot August afternoon while I sat there listening to Booker. I changed. That day, I became a different person. I became a prisoner just like the rest of them." Cleophus put the book on the shelf and I handed him the next one.

54.

THE MEETING WAS HELD out by the bleachers on the basketball court. Some of the inmates stood around while others sat on the grass. Booker stood in front of us with a pencil and notepad in his hand. Dill and Radio squatted beside him. Soupy and Newt were there and every now and again, I'd catch them looking my way. Booker looked at me and winked his eye; then he cleared his throat and went down the list of new fish.

"All right, gentlemen, let's make this quick. The first fish on the list is Stoney. He looks like a survivor to me. Do I have any prices on Stoney?" asked Booker.

"That's what you always say about the new fish," a man in the back said.

"Shut up," said Dill, popping gum.

"Do you want to put a price on Stoney or not?" asked Booker.

"Put me down for five dollars on the third week. It might take some time to make him crack," the man said. Booker handed Radio a slip of paper. Radio ran over to him and exchanged the paper for the money.

"I have five on three. Is there anybody else?"

"Give me ten on the fourth week," said Newt. Booker handed Dill a slip of paper and Dill ran and made the exchange.

"Okay, gentlemen, I've got ten dollars on the fourth week of this month. Any more on week four?" asked Booker. He looked around for any more hands to go up.

He looked at me. "Cleophus, don't you want to get in?" For a while, nobody made a sound. I felt sweat coming down my face. I had ten dollars left to my name. I really didn't want to gamble away any of it on whether or not a new fish was going to make it through his first month in prison. If I guessed the right week of the month, I could double my money, but if I guessed the wrong week, I'd lose every penny I had. If I didn't guess it all, who knew what Booker and his boys would do to me.

"Come on, Cleophus. You're one of us now," said Dill. He blew a bubble with the gum in his mouth and popped it.

"Yeah, you're one of us now," said Radio. Hearing this a second time made something snap in my mind. I thought about how long I was actually going to live my life behind bars. I had no family on the outside. I knew I needed to have one on the inside if I was going to make it in prison. I realized I couldn't make it in prison on my own. Every man sitting out there that day was my brother. I was a part of a family whether I liked it or not. I didn't have much of a choice. I had to make the best of a bad situation.

"Give me five on the fourth week," I said. Booker walked over and handed me the slip of paper with five over four on it and his signature. I handed him five dollars.

"All right, the next fish on the list is Digger." Before Booker could get Digger's name out of his mouth, everybody was calling out to him.

"Give me fifteen on the second week. He is already half-dead," somebody said.

"I want to put twenty on the second week."

"Put me down for twenty on the second, too." It went on like this until I realized that Digger was going to be more valuable to *the world dead than alive, and it didn't matter who he was or whether he believed in one god or four of them.*

55.

"DID YOU TELL HIM there was a price on his head?" I asked Cleophus as he stepped down off the ladder.

"You know I did. I told him everything."

"What did he say?"

"He just shrugged his shoulders. He didn't say anything. I told him to go down the cellblock line and buy himself a fork or something, but he shook his head. He told me there was no need. I asked him if he wanted to die. He said yes. And that's exactly what happened to him three days later in the shower."

"Who killed Digger?"

"Some folks said Booker had Dill and Radio kill Digger, but I really don't know for sure who killed Digger."

"Where were the guards?"

"Everywhere but where the action was. The guards knew Digger was going to be killed. Some of them even placed bets with Booker. They didn't care what happened as long as Booker gave them their cut. That's how things worked around here then, and that's how they work now."

"Those bastards are no good."

"There is something else I think you should know. I wasn't going to say anything, but I like you. I thought I wasn't going to, but I do."

"What is it?" I asked.

"There are prices on you too. They are some of the highest ones ever. I've tried to keep Booker and Moses off of you for as long as I could, but they are getting short on patience, and my standing with Boyer and the warden around here is starting to matter less and less to them. They'll kill me to get to you if they have to. And if you ain't scared, you should be. You could die."

"I'm not scared. I've never been scared a day in my life," I said.

"Every day is a good day to change, Sonny."

"Change for what? I didn't do anything. I haven't done one goddamn thing to anybody since the day I got here. Moses came after me; I didn't do anything to him."

"You didn't have to do anything. Every man who walks through those prison doors ends up paying a price for being here. I paid my price. Digger and Squeak paid their price. Now you have to pay yours. I can help you though, but you have to help me first."

"What do I have to do?" I asked.

"Come back to the storage with me and I'll show you."

"No way. I'm not playing games anymore," I told him.

"It's not a game. It's business. I'm trying to make the best of a bad situation. Sooner or later, we all have to."

"I'm not going back into that storage with you. Moses can do what he wants to me. He can kill me if he wants too. I'm not afraid to die."

"Are you sure?" Cleophus asked me.

"I'm damn sure!"

"You can't say you didn't have a choice. You could have had it easy in here. I could have taken care of you," said Cleophus.

"I don't need anybody to take care of me. I can take care of myself."

"I guess we'll just have to see about that."

I stood alone in the stacks while Cleophus went over to the desk to talk to Boyer. I avoided him as much as I could. Then Briggs came to take us to the dining hall.

56.

I ASKED BRIGGS to escort me to my cell because I wasn't hungry. I was too scared to go to the dining hall. Moses and his boys knew I'd have to leave my cell sooner or later. They grabbed me on my way to my work detail about two days later. They dragged me into the shower with my mouth covered. They held me down while Moses raped me. When he was done, he told them to finish me off while he watched. They busted up my head and broke my nose. They cracked the bones in my right leg in so many places the doctors had to put pins in it to hold it together. I spent over a month in the infirmary, and I had to work with a special nurse to learn how to walk again.

The only person who came to visit me was Chaplain Gregory. He was a short man, but he always looked happy and at peace with himself. He came to sit at my bedside every day I spent in the infirmary. Chaplain Gregory told me that I screamed in my sleep. He asked me what was troubling me. I told him about the nightmares that I had been having since I came to the infirmary. In my dreams, I kept seeing Cabbage drowning in blood. I could hear him screaming my name. I told Chaplain Gregory the truth about what happened to Cabbage. He held my hand and told me I could be reborn in the name of Christ and be forgiven for all of my sins. I asked him what I needed to do. He told me to surrender my life to Christ. So I gave my life over to Christ before I was released from the infirmary. I got baptized. I went to the chapel for the Sunday services and I prayed. I prayed that one day I would be able to walk again, and I prayed that I would make parole.

Soon I started feeling like a new person. I slept at night and I didn't have nightmares about Cabbage. I went to therapy classes, and I soon learned to stand up on my own without crutches. When I learned to walk without them, I walked much slower and I dragged my right leg. The inmates patted me on my shoulder and congratulated me when I passed them. Inmates I had seen a hundred times but didn't know offered to help me along when they saw me coming. I wouldn't let them help me. The man who walked in prison really had to walk alone. I bet that sounds like something you'd expect Cleophus to say, but I was starting to come up with proverbs of my own.

I didn't see Cleophus after I got out of the infirmary. Chaplain Gregory helped me get a job transfer, and I worked with him in the Prison Ministry. The job didn't require me to stand. My job was to counsel the new fish. Most of them weren't much interested in letting Christ into their lives, but Chaplain

Gregory said nothing changed a man's heart like time. He asked me how I liked working in ministry. I told him that it was all still new, but I was glad I didn't have to work in the library with Cleophus. He wasn't the kind of person I thought I needed to be around. Plus, he wasn't a Christian. I finally saw him in the dining hall, but we didn't speak. Chaplain Gregory told me that I should forgive him. I did, because nothing killed a heart quicker than bitterness.

By the time I went up for parole, I had told more new fish than I could count the story about how I ended up in the Sparta State Prison. Most of the new fish survived in prison with few problems. Some of them didn't. Inmates still placed bets on whether certain new fish would make it through the first month in prison or not. But I never bet. I wanted to walk into my parole hearing with a clean record. I went in and sat in front of the Parole Committee. There were seven of them. Five of them were men and two were women. All of them looked stiff and serious. They had a whole lot of questions to ask me while they flipped through folders and passed papers. The man in the dark suit and tie in the middle seat asked me the final question. He asked me if I was ready to enter back into society. I said yes, and I told him that I had found Christ. He looked at me and smiled. The committee declined my parole.

57.

SOMEONE TOLD CLEOPHUS that I was declined. He walked over and sat beside me on one of the benches in the exercise yard. He told me I shouldn't be too upset about not getting paroled. He said that most inmates never got it on the first try. He told me I would make parole in no time if I stayed on the straight and narrow and passed the high school equivalency test. I told him I didn't make parole because I hadn't repented for all of my sins. He looked over at me and laughed. I told him I needed to face the truth about why I was in prison.

"Prison ain't the place where a man ought to dwell on the truth too much, especially if he wants to survive," he said.

"Maybe, everybody's not meant to survive."

"There you go sounding like Digger, but at least you're still alive."

"I'm alive because of Christ."

"Well, I don't have much to say about that."

"You don't have to say anything. It's true."

"Well, everybody needs to believe in something."

"Do you remember that story I told you in the library?"

"You mean the one about how you ended up in prison?"

"That's it. It was a lie. You knew it all along, but I wanted to confess."

"Thanks. It takes a big man to own up to a lie. You know where to find me whenever you're ready to tell me what really happened. I'll listen. That's what friends do."

"You're not the kind of friend I would tell. Your story almost got me killed, remember."

"I didn't intend for it to do that. I told you that story to help you, but you didn't believe it," said Cleophus. "A story is about more than just the story."

"You're right, and friendship is about more than just the friends." I stood up and shook his hand. I walked out into the middle of the exercise yard. I looked up to the sky. I closed my eyes, and I said a prayer for Cabbage.

58.

THIS STORY JUST wouldn't end right unless I explained why I got sentenced to do ten years in the Sparta State Prison. It took me a long time to own up to the part I played in helping Cabbage rob old Potter's store. What I have left to say won't be as exciting as what I have already said. Telling the truth can be a pretty dull business, but I thought I should end by telling the real story straight and let you choose to believe what you want to believe and leave the rest behind.

59.

IT MIGHT BE EASIER now for you to understand why I wished I had been the one who died in that motorcar accident instead of Daisy. I didn't find it strange at all when I overheard some of the prison guards who lived in Moon County say most women were glad Daisy was dead. I figured they just didn't like her because she was pretty. Daisy had thick brows, and her eyes were big and serious. She dropped out of high school and started staying out late. She drank gin straight and smoked reefer cigarettes with men much older than she was. The rumor was that she slept with men for money and that she had a nasty woman's disease. I never knew if the rumor was true or not, but Cabbage and Daisy ended up going together after Uncle Tuck put him out of his house for coming home doped up all the time.

Cabbage was really my older brother, and in a lot of ways he was the closet thing I had to a daddy besides my Uncle Tuck. My real daddy left home before I was born. When I was young, Cabbage told me all kinds of stories about him. He always called Daddy Will in the stories he told me. Momma named Cabbage after my daddy, but she gave him a nickname because of the birthmark on his forehead. The birthmark got Cabbage so much attention that I wanted one for myself. I wanted to go everywhere he went and do everything he did. Then one day, Momma told me that Cabbage's stories were not true; Cabbage was barely two years old when Daddy left home.

Momma hardly ever talked about Daddy. Sometimes at night I could hear her crying in her room while she said her prayers. I asked Cabbage why momma prayed and cried so much. He told me she cried because she wanted to make things better than what they were for us. There were always more problems than money. Momma cooked, cleaned, and sewed for other people until women were allowed to work at the cotton mill, and she was hired to work there. It didn't pay much, but it kept us from having to depend on our relatives all the time.

Uncle Tuck was my momma's oldest brother, and he always called her Sister instead of Mary. He was married to my Aunt Bea and they had a daughter named Colleen. She got married to a minister's son and moved to Chattanooga. What little we learned about her after that, we learned from the letters she sent to Aunt Bea and Uncle Tuck. Uncle Tuck delivered ice for a living. He didn't have much, but he always made a point of coming over and checking on Momma to see if she had everything she needed.

Aunt Bea took care of the house. We always spent Christmas Day there. My daddy's sister, Aunt Ellen, would drive all the way from Atlanta with her husband, Uncle Roger. They'd be all dressed up in fancy clothes. Aunt Ellen and Uncle Roger gave me and Cabbage peppermint candy and a dollar apiece for Christmas. One Christmas, Aunt Ellen walked in wearing a velvet dress. Momma made such a fuss over that velvet dress that Aunt Ellen took it off and let Momma wear it until it was time for them to leave. That was just one of the few times that I ever remember my momma being happy. I believed that if we bought Momma a velvet dress like Aunt Ellen's she'd be happy forever. But I knew it would cost more than the two dollars and change me and Cabbage had between the two of us at the time.

Cabbage said he knew a way to get Momma a velvet dress, and it wouldn't cost us any money at all; we were going to steal it from Mrs. Cush's dress shop on Main Street. But old Potter caught Cabbage stealing out of his store again, and he decided to press charges with the sheriff. We thought he might drop them like he did so many times before, after Momma went to talk to him. But he didn't. Cabbage was locked up in the reformatory for a year.

60.

WHEN HE COULD, Uncle Tuck drove me and Momma over to the reformatory to visit Cabbage. Uncle Tuck drove through the gate. The guard checked his identification and directed him to the parking lot for visitors. Fences were wrapped around all the different dormitories. They were only connected by concrete walkways. Cabbage was only allowed to receive two visitors, so Uncle Tuck sat in the waiting area in the main building. Momma said they must have been feeding Cabbage pretty well because he had put on weight after being in for only a few weeks. He smiled and laughed like he was really glad to see us. He didn't like the clothes they made him wear, and he said the place always smelled like rotten onions. He had made a couple of friends, but he didn't trust them.

When Uncle Tuck drove me and Momma over to see Cabbage the second time, he was missing two front teeth on the right side of his mouth. Unlike before, his hands were cuffed and a guard stood behind him. He told Momma that he was learning how to box, and he had gotten into a brawl with one of the older boys. Momma worried, but Cabbage said that we should have seen what he did to that boy. I asked Cabbage what did he do to him. Cabbage told me he almost knocked his head off his shoulders. I asked Cabbage if he would teach me how to box when he got out. He told me that he would.

Cabbage told me that he had plenty of stories to tell me about the reformatory in his next letter. He made me promise I would write him back just as soon as I got his letter in the mail. Before we left that day, Momma warned Cabbage not to misbehave. She kept coughing, even when she was trying to speak. She rubbed her hands and used them to cover her mouth when she coughed. Cabbage asked her what was wrong. She told him she was probably coming down with a virus. What Cabbage didn't know was that Momma had been coughing like that for months, and the tonic she took wasn't working. Momma said that she would go see the doctor, but I knew she said it just to keep Cabbage from worrying about her. Cabbage looked at me and told me to take care of Momma. He made me cross my heart and hope to die like he did when we were small. It seemed silly to me at the time, but I did it.

The last time we went to visit Cabbage in the reformatory, Uncle Tuck let me drive the motorcar half the way there. He taught Cabbage how to drive just before he got locked up in the reformatory. Momma asked him if he would teach me. When the guard brought Cabbage in, we hardly recognized him.

Uncle Tuck got so mad he balled up his fists. All I could do was stare at Cabbage. His hands were cuffed and his head was bald. He had lost so much weight you could see his jaw bones. His bottom lip was swollen, and on the left side of his face was a dark bruise. He sat in his chair slouched over. He looked down at the floor. He mumbled and laughed like he was doped up. Uncle Tuck asked the guard what happened to him, and the guard shrugged his shoulders. Cabbage asked where Momma was. Hoping to change the subject, I asked him why he stopped answering my letters. He asked me where Momma was again, and Uncle Tuck told me I had better tell him the truth. Cabbage looked up at me. I told him about the tests the doctor did, and that Momma had cancer. He just kept staring at me until tears came rolling down his face. He stood up, and the guard stepped forward to lead him to the door. Uncle Tuck told Cabbage he was going to have the church pray for him. I called out his name. He looked back over his shoulder at me; then he walked through the open door and the guard closed it behind him.

61.

I DIDN'T TELL CABBAGE that the doctor told Momma he didn't think she was going to live very long. She got so sick she couldn't get out of the bed to go to work. Aunt Bea came over and cooked and cleaned, and gave Momma her bath. I sat at the kitchen table doing homework and listening to them whispering about who was going to pay the rent on the house.

I got up early the next morning, and instead of going to school, I followed the line of folks walking to work at the cotton mill. I asked one of them where I could find Mr. Granger, the head supervisor. The man pointed to him standing down by the door of an office trying to kill flies with a fly swatter. He walked into the office and I followed him. I walked up to the desk where he was counting some pennies and stacking them in front of him. I had never seen so many pennies in my life. I asked him if he could give me a job. He looked at me like he wasn't sure he heard what I was asking him. I told him my Momma worked for him, and she had to quit because she was sick with cancer. I figured I could take her place. He frowned and told me I was too young to work at the cotton mill, and that I should be in school. Just before I walked out of the door, he told me that I might try old Potter because he was always looking for somebody like me to help him around his store.

I knew old Potter would never hire me after what Cabbage did, but I had to take a chance. I walked into the store that morning and old Potter stood behind the counter in an apron, counting bullets. No one else was in the store except the two of us and an old drunk man wearing dirty clothes. I had never seen him around Moon County before. He kept asking old Potter on which aisle he could find the things he wanted. Old Potter looked at me and asked me why I wasn't in school. I told him I was looking for a job. He told me I was looking in the wrong place for a job because he couldn't afford to pay anybody, with times being as hard as they were in Moon County. And if he could hire somebody, he didn't think it would be me, especially not after what Cabbage did. Old Potter asked me how my Momma was coming along. I told him that the doctor said that things didn't look too good for her. He asked me how I was doing in school. I told him the teacher said that I was doing fine. He wiped his eye with one of his hands. Then he told me to go talk to Mrs. Wick and tell her that he sent me. The summer auction she held every year to raise money for the reformatory was coming up, and she always hired a few boys to help clean her backyard and set up the tables and chairs.

62.

MRS. WICK'S HOUSE was bigger than the county courthouse, but it needed to be painted. I knocked on the door and Sofia, her maid, answered it. Two cats ran past me. They scared me a little and I was already nervous. I told Sofia why I was there. She told me to go around to the back porch because that's where Mrs. Wick was. The yard was big like a park and full of trees and thick bushes. When I got to the back porch, I saw Mrs. Wick.

Mrs. Wick was wearing a summer hat. Sofia talked to her while she watered the potted plants. She came down the stairs and looked at me. She put down her water bucket and took her hat off of her head. Her hair fell to her shoulders. She told me to turn around so that she could get a good look at me. She made me hold out my hands, and she told me I needed to clean my fingernails. She asked me how much experience I had with yard work. I told her I had a lot of experience. She asked me which days I was able to work. I told her every day. Mrs. Wick looked at me hard. She asked me what about school. I told her that I would quit if she gave me the job. Sofia stood on the porch laughing with her hand over her mouth. Mrs. Wick shook her head and asked God to bless my soul. She said she would try me out for a few weeks to see whether she liked me or not.

63.

IN THE MEANTIME, Momma was getting sicker. The medicine the doctor gave her made her weak and sleepy. Aunt Bea wouldn't let her take any tonic. The food Aunt Bea fed her would find its way back out and into the bucket we kept by the bed. The most Aunt Bea could get Momma to eat was pea soup. Aunt Bea said it helped her to sleep. Whenever she woke up, Momma always asked about Cabbage. I never told her what me and Uncle Tuck saw when we last visited Cabbage. I knew I couldn't tell her about all the times we went to visit Cabbage after that, and he wouldn't come out to see us. Uncle Tuck said Cabbage was just being stubborn. I told Momma Cabbage was fine, and that he'd gotten so fat she'd hardly recognize him when he came home. Then I talked about myself. I told her I was working for Mrs. Wick. I asked her if that was okay. She said it was as long as I kept my grades up in school. I promised her I would. I watched as her head tilted off to the side and she closed her eyes. I walked out the door and went into the kitchen where I saw Aunt Bea sitting at the table with Uncle Tuck. She was crying.

Uncle Tuck told me to sit down at the table. I could tell he had something serious to say to me. He told me he didn't think

Momma was going to be able to hang on much longer. He and Aunt Bea said that they had a talk with Momma about what might be best for my future. Momma told them she wanted me to go live with Aunt Ellen and Uncle Roger because things would be better for me if I got out of Moon County. Uncle Tuck asked me if I would like living in Atlanta. Before I could say anything, Aunt Bea told me that it was a nice place to live and there were lots of things for a boy my age to do there. I asked them what was going to happen to Cabbage. After all, he was going to be getting out of the reformatory soon. I asked Uncle Tuck if Cabbage would be coming with me to live in Atlanta. He said that Cabbage was almost a grown man and he wasn't as worried about him as he was about me. Aunt Bea looked at me and told me not to worry about Cabbage. He was going to be just fine in Moon County.

64.

I WENT TO Mrs. Wick's house to clean her yard after school let out. When I wasn't working in the yard, she had me running errands for her and Sofia. I started to think that Mrs. Wick liked me just fine because she invited me into the parlor to sit with her when there was no yard work or any errands to run. I really liked sitting with Mrs. Wick in the parlor.

One afternoon, Sofia brought in a sandwich and a glass of milk for me and tea for Mrs. Wick. We sat in the chairs by the tall windows. Mrs. Wick asked me all about school and my family. I told her I was doing fine in school. I told her about Momma being sick, but I didn't tell her about Cabbage being in the reformatory. She told me about her tea set collection. Mrs. Wick always asked Sofia to bring her pills whenever she talked about her husband, Culver, and their son, Albert. Talking about them gave her really bad headaches. Albert died in a motorcar accident while he was in college up North. Her husband fell down the stairs and died two months after that.

I don't think Mrs. Wick ever got over losing her son in that accident. She put a lock on his bedroom door upstairs, and she had Sofia change his bed sheets once a week. Sometimes, Mrs.

Wick fell asleep in her chair while telling me a story, and she woke up asking me to go and ask Sofia where Albert had gone. Sofia told me to tell her that he was up on Main Street, and he would be right back. Once I told Sofia that Albert was nowhere around, and she told me to do as I was told or she'd make sure I didn't get my week's pay. So I told Mrs. Wick what Sofia told me to tell her. That always calmed Mrs. Wick down enough for her to tell me another one of her stories. The stories got so long that sometimes they'd have to be continued on another day.

As the time for the auction came near, I did less and less yard work. I just sat around with Mrs. Wick most of the time and listened. Her favorite story was the story that she used to tell about the masked magician she hired for one of Albert's birthday parties. I knew how much she loved telling that story. She always asked me if she had ever told it to me before. I said no, even though I had heard her tell it many times. She'd tell me the whole story from the beginning to the end, and every now and again, she'd interrupt the story and tell me how much she wished I could have been there to see it for myself.

65.

THERE WERE a few days when I couldn't go to Mrs. Wick's house at all. Momma had gotten so sick I didn't want to leave her. Aunt Bea had practically moved into our house. I kept expecting Aunt Ellen and Uncle Roger to come, but they never came to visit while Momma was sick. Uncle Tuck and I drove out to the reformatory, thinking Cabbage might want to know how Momma was doing, but he refused the visitation. When we got home, Momma asked about Cabbage. Uncle Tuck said that it did no good telling her the truth, so I lied and told her that Cabbage was fine, and that he'd gotten so fat she'd hardly recognize him when he came home. She asked me when he was coming home. I told her he said he would be coming home soon. I held her hand until she fell asleep.

Momma never woke up. We had the funeral and buried her in the graveyard next to her oldest sister. Everybody kept asking about Cabbage. He was granted a leave to attend Momma's funeral with two guards, but he refused to take it. Uncle Tuck and I drove over to find out why Cabbage wasn't coming to the funeral, but he refused the visitation again. Uncle Tuck tried to demand they let us see Cabbage, but we were told that Cabbage had the right to refuse visitation.

The day before the funeral, Uncle Tuck sat at the kitchen table explaining the whole situation to the family. Aunt Bea cried. Aunt Ellen complained about Cabbage. She said he was acting worse than a stubborn rooster, and it was a shame the way he was turning his back on Momma. She told Aunt Bea that Cabbage was just like our daddy. When she said that, I called her an old hen, and I told her to shut up because Cabbage was a million times better than our daddy. Aunt Ellen squeezed her pocketbook close to her chest and looked at Uncle Roger who was frowning at me. Uncle Roger asked me if I said what he thought he heard me say. I just looked at him without saying a word. Aunt Bea asked me what had gotten into me. Uncle Tuck told me that I owed Aunt Ellen an apology for what I said, but I never said a word. Aunt Ellen said that if that was the type of ungrateful behavior she could expect from me after she had opened the doors of her house, then maybe it might be best if I stayed in Moon County until I learned how to act like a gentleman. Aunt Ellen and Uncle Roger drove back to Atlanta after my momma's funeral and I never saw them again.

66.

MRS. WICK TOLD ME how sorry she was that my mother had passed. She told me she'd understand if I didn't want to help her get the yard ready for the auction, but I told her I didn't mind. It would take my mind off the fact that Momma was dead and I had to live with Uncle Tuck and Aunt Bea until I finished school. Knowing the auction was coming up was just about as exciting as knowing that it was getting closer to the time when Cabbage would be coming home. I had never been to an auction, especially not one where they sold fancy merchandise.

Mrs. Wick had hired all kinds of people to cook and serve the food, and even bring in tables and chairs. I had finished cleaning the yard the day before, so I was mostly helping to set up the tables and chairs in the backyard. Mrs. Wick went around straightening the tablecloths; then she showed the musicians where they could set up. I went up to the kitchen door to ask Sofia for a drink of water. I watched Sofia search through kitchen cabinets while she ordered the cooks around the kitchen and complained about being overworked. She said she was too busy trying to find the new tea set for Mrs. Wick's afternoon tea with the auction committee. Sofia told me to wash my hands and get the glass of water myself. I stood in a corner of the porch sipping water and watching everybody move like busy bees. Two motorcars pulled up into the yard, and Mrs. Wick went over to greet them. I went back to helping set up the tables and chairs. But I couldn't keep from staring at Mrs. Wick's company dressed in such fancy clothes.

I recognized the woman in the hat with all the feathers right away. It was Mrs. Cush. She was with her husband. Mr. Cush stood beside the motorcar with his arms out while Mrs. Cush laid two pretty dresses across his arm. I remember thinking how much my momma would have liked them if she had been able to see them. A tall man got out of the other motorcar. He walked with a cane while he held another one in his hand. Mrs. Wick kissed them all on the cheek and escorted them to the porch to sit down. Mrs. Wick called Sofia's name, but Sofia never came. Another motorcar pulled up behind the others, and old Potter got out carrying a shotgun. He looked out across the yard at me. I pretended I didn't see him. He joined the others on the porch and they talked and laughed. Mrs. Wick called Sofia's name again. This time her voice sounded like her patience had gotten short. Then I heard a man's voice calling my name. It was old Potter.

I got really nervous and my legs wouldn't move. Old Potter called out my name again and waved me over. I put down the chair I held and walked toward the porch slowly. I saw the dresses laying across the back of the chair next to the door to the kitchen. The cane and shotgun were standing against the house.

Mrs. Wick and her visitors were all sitting around the table. They all stared at me except Mrs. Wick. She looked down. I saw that she was rubbing her hands the way Momma did that day we went to visit Cabbage in the reformatory. The sweat on my skin started to feel cold. Old Potter reached over and patted my arm, and he told them all how proud he was of the work that I was doing for Mrs. Wick and how he had hoped that it would keep me from ending up in the reformatory like my brother Cabbage.

He told the entire story about how Cabbage ended up in the reformatory, and how raising money for the reformatory was benefiting young men like him who got started on the wrong track in life. I stood there as long as I could listening to old Potter tell his story. My hands sweated. I felt myself backing away in shame, and when I turned around to run, I bumped into Sofia. The tray she held in her hands fell and the tea set broke. I ran as fast as I could, and I never went back. I hadn't realized until then that a lot of folks in Moon County were looking at me and seeing Cabbage.

67.

WHEN CABBAGE FINALLY came home, we all pretended not to notice how different he was. I figured he didn't want to smile much, because of his missing teeth, but his hair had grown back and he had regained some of his weight. Aunt Bea cooked a big dinner, and she made a cake and put candles on it to celebrate the homecoming. Cabbage sat at the table and ate, but he kept looking down at his plate the whole time. He never lifted his head or said a word. He spent the rest of the day in his room. At first, Cabbage wouldn't say anything to me. Then he started to open up and told me stories about the reformatory. I tried to get Cabbage to teach me how to box, but he kept saying no. I started to think that maybe he didn't know how to box at all. All he wanted to do was sit in his room and stare out the window. He kept all of his belongings under the bed in the box he brought them in when he came from the reformatory. Aunt Bea fussed at him about taking regular baths and changing his clothes.

Uncle Tuck questioned him about not showing up for the job he got for him delivering ice. Uncle Tuck said Cabbage wasn't trying to look for work. I could tell that Uncle Tuck was running out of patience. I asked him to give Cabbage more time to get used to things.

As that year passed, Cabbage started going out more, and then he was gone all the time and we hardly saw him. I waited up for him at night. Sometimes he came home. Most times he didn't. It got to the point that when he did come home, he was always drunk and dirty. Uncle Tuck tolerated as much as he could before he asked Cabbage to leave. That's when Cabbage started living with Daisy in a little house that a cousin of hers let her stay in while the cousin was over in Sparta County taking care of her sick sister.

After a few days passed, I went over to Daisy's cousin's house to see how Cabbage was doing. He and Daisy were doped up on reefer cigarettes and gin. Cabbage tried to get me to try both, but I wouldn't do it. The whole thing just felt wrong to me. Cabbage told me he had gotten a job working as a cook at the café on Main Street. He said it didn't pay him much, but it was a job. I told him that Uncle Tuck and Aunt Bea said hello. They really didn't, but it seemed like the right thing to say at the time. Cabbage didn't say anything after that. In fact, there wasn't much he could say, because he dozed off on Daisy's shoulder. She looked over at me half-dazed and smiled. She told me that maybe I should come back the next day. Cabbage didn't have to work.

When I dropped by the next day after school, I walked up on the porch and knocked on the screened door. I heard Daisy scream that she was in the back. I walked around to the back porch. She was sitting in a house dress I could see through. Cabbage was nowhere around. Daisy never took her eyes off me while she rubbed together the clothes she had in her washtub. She asked me if Cabbage had the same daddy as I did. I told her he did. I asked her why she wanted to know. She said she just wondered because we seemed so different. She caught me staring at her chest. She asked me if I'd ever seen a naked woman before. I told her I had seen a lot of naked women. Daisy laughed and called me a liar. She got up and walked into the house. I sat on the steps watching the sky.

Daisy came out with a cup and a bottle of gin in a wrinkled paper sack. She handed me the cup. Gin was in it. She told me that life would seem sweeter if I didn't try to sip it so fast. After I took a sip, I started to cough. Daisy laughed and rubbed the collar of a shirt together. She said I'd get used to it after a while. Daisy told me that Cabbage drank every day, and he spent most of his money on reefer cigarettes. Those cigarettes made him talk crazy. When he got doped up, he talked about killing folks and Momma's funeral. Daisy said Cabbage blamed himself for Momma's death. I told her Momma died of cancer. Daisy said I should try getting Cabbage to believe that.

68.

THEN DAISY TOLD ME something that I didn't want to believe. Cabbage was planning to leave Moon County. She thought maybe he had told me he was planning to go, but Cabbage hardly told me anything after he came home from the reformatory.

That day on her porch, Daisy told me Cabbage's plan. He was planning to rob old Potter, and take the money and leave Moon County. Cabbage believed old Potter owed him for the year he spent in the reformatory. I asked Daisy how Cabbage was planning to leave when he didn't have a motorcar. This was how I came into the plan. He was going to have me steal Uncle Tuck's motorcar. I told Daisy I would never do that. She took the bottle out of the sack and poured more gin into the cup. She took one sip from the cup and laughed. Cabbage told her I would do whatever he told me to do.

I stayed away from Daisy's cousin's house because I didn't want to see Cabbage. I thought about what Daisy told me more than I wanted to. It was like a fever that just stayed with me. I tried to tell myself that everything Daisy said was not true, but

Cabbage had bought a gun. She showed it to me before I left that day. I was convinced. Daisy knew more about Cabbage than I did, and I had known him my whole life. Plus, I was scared. I didn't know exactly what I would say if Cabbage actually came to me and asked me to take Uncle Tuck's motorcar.

That day came sooner than I thought. Cabbage came to Uncle Tuck's house after he and Aunt Bea had gone to church. Cabbage knew I hardly ever went to church. I sat at the kitchen table watching him stuff his mouth with cold chicken and sip gin out of the flask he pulled out of his back pocket. I could tell he was going to talk about leaving Moon County just by the way he looked at me. He started telling me about his plans to rob old Potter's store, and about the gun he bought from the man who sold him reefer cigarettes. I didn't say anything. I didn't know what to say. That was the most alive I had seen Cabbage since he came back from the reformatory. Everything he said was so full of hope. The three of us were going to go to Atlanta. We were finally going to get a good start in life. I asked him what if we got caught. Cabbage said we wouldn't. Daisy would be waiting for us behind the wheel, and we would just drive away without stopping. I asked him about Uncle Tuck's motorcar. Cabbage said just as soon as we got on our feet we'd send him money to get a new one. He said Uncle Tuck had been delivering ice so long his boss would let him drive the ice truck whenever he wanted to. But that still didn't make what we were doing feel right to me. Cabbage said nothing in life was right and that you had to take whatever you wanted in the world because nobody was going to give you anything. Cabbage wanted me to go with him to Momma's grave. We spent the rest of that day in the graveyard sipping gin and smoking reefer cigarettes, and thinking about how things used to be and how much better they were going to get.

69.

TWO WEEKS LATER, I slipped out of the house early. I had a few of my belongings in a bag and the keys to Uncle Tuck's motorcar. I put the motorcar in gear the way Cabbage told me.

I pushed it out of the yard and started the engine when I got out by the road. I drove to Daisy's house. The two of them waited on the front porch with two suitcases and the box Cabbage brought from the reformatory. Cabbage drove to old Potter's store.

Old Potter opened the doors to the store at seven o'clock every morning except Sundays. Cabbage and I walked into the store. Daisy waited in the motorcar around the corner. I had noticed her hands shaking just before I got out. Cabbage had told her that all she had to do was drive as fast as she could once we got into the motorcar with the money. Daisy nodded. She took a swallow from the flask she had sitting on her lap. She handed it to Cabbage and Cabbage handed it to me. He told me it would help calm my nerves.

Old Potter counted money at the register. He asked me why I was in the store so early. He didn't say anything to Cabbage at first. We hadn't been in his store that early in the morning in a long time. We told him we needed to pick up a few things for a trip. Old Potter asked Cabbage if he could help him with anything. Cabbage didn't say a word. He pulled his gun out and pointed it at old Potter. Old Potter stopped counting his money. He told Cabbage he could take anything he wanted as long as he didn't shoot him. Cabbage told him to clear out the drawer of the register and give the money to me in a sack. Old Potter did what Cabbage told him to do. I walked over and stood by the door with the money, but Cabbage wouldn't move; he stared at old Potter. Old Potter started sweating. He told Cabbage he was making a mistake and that he could make a better life for himself if he just worked hard. Cabbage told old Potter he didn't believe that anymore, and that he felt really sorry for anybody who did. I walked over to pull Cabbage to the door. When Cabbage turned his back to walk out behind me, old Potter shot him. Cabbage dropped to the floor with the gun still in his hand. I thought that old Potter was going to shoot me, too, but he didn't. I ran to the motorcar.

70.

DAISY DROVE Uncle Tuck's motorcar as fast as it could go. She was so nervous she could barely steady her arm enough to get the flask to her mouth. She never asked me about Cabbage, but I could tell by her tears that she knew what had happened. It was slowly settling in her like the gin. I wanted to say something to her. I wanted to tell her that Cabbage was okay, but it would not have done either one of us any good to hear a lie. I remember seeing Daisy lose control of the motorcar just before we crossed the county line. The motorcar skidded off the road and down a hill. It ran through a few trees and crashed into one of them.

I woke up in the hospital. There was a thick bandage around my head. I saw the sheriff standing next to the doctor. The doctor said I was lucky, and if he didn't know better, he'd almost think I had died and come back alive. I asked him about Daisy. He said that she died instantly. The sheriff walked into the room and told me my Uncle Tuck and Aunt Bea wanted to see me. I refused the visitation.

ABOUT THE AUTHOR

J.K. DENNIS was born in Milledgeville, Georgia. He is an Assistant Professor of English at Forest Park College. He lives in Ballwin, Missouri. Questions and comments about the book can be sent to 9lessons@3HP.us.